Jewels of Light

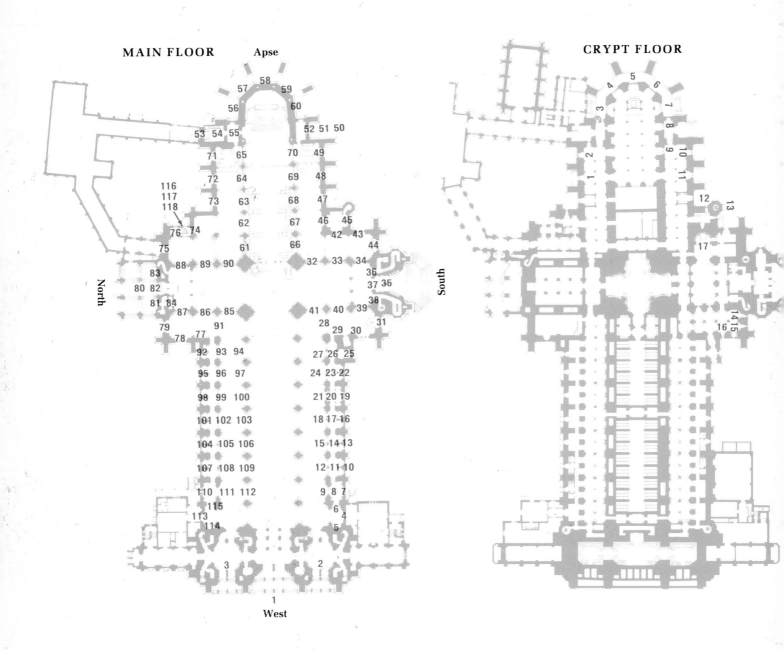

Jewels of Light

THE STAINED GLASS AND MOSAICS OF WASHINGTON CATHEDRAL

edited by: Nancy S. Montgomery and Marcia P. Johnson

THE CATHEDRAL CHURCH
OF SAINT PETER AND SAINT PAUL
MOUNT SAINT ALBAN
WASHINGTON, DISTRICT OF COLUMBIA

"Jewels of Light"

Cover: Detail of Creation (West) Rose Window

Photographers

Del Ankers	Robert Lautman
Morton Broffman	W. L. Mahon
Hal H. Conroy	Schulz
James R. Dunlop	Stewart Brothers, Inc.
Fay Photo Service	Irwin Wensink
Horydczak	

The right lancet of the Universal Peace window

CONTENTS

SIGNS AND SYMBOLS
OF STAINED GLASS

The stained glass windows of Washington Cathedral not only create an ambience for the architecture but also are an integral part of it, constituting a major portion of the enclosure walls. From the exterior they are seen only as walls of black glass broken by lead lines and do not appear to have the capacity to flood the interior with beautifully colored light. However, this is precisely the reason for luminous colored glass.

The first cathedral windows for Bethlehem Chapel were created and fabricated in England, as were a number of the small windows in the crypt aisles outside this chapel. These windows are typical of fifteenth century English glass, with much ornate decorative design work surrounding the principal figures. This style is also characterized by very white flesh tones, white drapery, a large amount of green glass, with less blue and red glass.

After the installation of the first English windows, cathedral authorities engaged in an extended debate about future glass. Once they concluded that what they sought was glass of the French style, rich in primary colors, they came to the following mandates:

- *The windows should be rich in color and rich in scale*
- *They should be radiant sources of light to secure adequate daytime illumination of the cathedral*
- *They should be vivid in form and feeling and emotionally expressive as well as splendidly decorative*
- *Each window should be designed to harmonize with its architectural opening and clearly reveal the shape of the stonework*
- *Each window must also be in pleasing harmony with adjacent windows*
- *The drawing, design and details of the glass should attempt to achieve an impression of sincerity, vitality, strength and legibility*
- *In terms of scale, the artist must consider the placement of each window with its distance from the viewer. Tall clerestory openings high above eye level must feature elongated figures to withstand the foreshortening effect when viewed from the floor.*

In many respects the cathedral's glorious windows resemble a composition in music. Each window is a single note in a symphony which will take eighty years

ation (West) Rose

Detail of the Epiphany window in Bethlehem Chapel, among the oldest glass in the cathedral

to complete. It must be different from other notes, but not too different, for then it becomes a discord. When this cathedral symphony is completed there will be two hundred and fourteen notes—or windows.

Since the cathedral's construction began, it has been the Building Committee that has passed collective judgment on each artist's design and decided on its fitness for inclusion in the symphony.

An important secondary aspect in the creation of the symphony is the imagery, known to cathedral builders as the iconography. Without a predetermined iconographic roadmap, each window would become a random collection of ideas, and the cathedral a veritable scrapbook. To avoid such unfortunate confusion, the cathedral's first dean, aided by the Building Committee and endorsed by the Cathedral Chapter, devised and set forth an iconographic plan for most of the future windows.

As the years have passed, succeeding deans and Building Committees have modified and added flesh to the first bare-bones iconography. As the composition has come closer to completion, window opening by window opening, there has been a steady growth in the combination of notes and chords in the total symphony.

What are these thematic concepts and what are they trying to convey? They are proclaiming segments of the biblical and historic Christian church, including its saints, martyrs, missionaries, leaders and teachers through the centuries. Some medieval cathedrals attempted to include everything in their symbolism; this is not the case with Washington Cathedral.

Washington Cathedral's glass and sculpture strive to convey the message that everything was created by the God we worship and in the fullness of time he sent his incarnate son to become our salvation. "The word was made flesh and dwelt among us."

The viewer must keep in mind that each window is but a part of the total cathedral plan. The themes predetermined the individual motif for each window. In some cases, such as Bethlehem and Children's Chapels, the art is totally related to and in fact announces the chapel theme.

Since a window is a mosaic of glass pieces held together by lead cames, it is appropriate to refer in this guide book to the superb mosaics in Resurrection Chapel. Composed of reflecting glass tessera, the large panel above the altar is the artist's stylized concept of the Resurrection. The six wall mosaics begin with the Easter morning Mary Magdalene recognition of her master, and symbolize succeeding post-resurrection events with the final panel in the rear wall recalling the Ascension of Christ. These mosaics tell the story of the chapel. They are stunningly beautiful in an interior chapel without any daylight.

The symbolism of the stained glass windows in the main body of the cathedral begins with the glorious rose window in the west facade at the west end of the nave. It paints in abstract the artist's version of the creation of the universe and has at its very center the small white light that shines to the far borders of the universe.

A window of abstract design can, by selection and movement of colors, suggest great themes as clearly as one of traditional representation. A rose window is the triumph of the Gothic architect's skill; however, because of its many subdivisions it is almost impossible for the glass artist to create discernible figures, especially in a church as vast as Washington Cathedral. In the south and north roses, the figures are so small as to be undecipherable with the naked eye.

The nave clerestory windows to the east of the rose pick up the biblical story after creation and suggest great themes of Old Testament history with the Hebrews as God's chosen people. Different versions of the same theme are portrayed in the north and south windows. [At this writing not all of these windows

have been designed and installed, hence the temporary opaque glass.] The first pair, closest to the west rose, shows the earth as man's shelter given by God. The second pair recalls God's covenant with the Hebrews. The next pair characterizes the passage of time and history in the Hebrew nation's growth. The fourth pair records how the people sinned and were brought to redemption through purification and reformation. The great faith of the Hebrews is personified in the sixth pair. Prophets foretell a messiah in the seventh bay, with salvation foretold in the eighth. In the ninth or easternmost pair the conversions and ministry of the apostles Peter and Paul, patron saints of Washington Cathedral, create the transition from Old Testament to New Testament imagery for the transepts and choir.

The west rose and all nave clerestory windows are being created by the same artist, according to the guidelines laid down by the Building Committee. They are very luminous, without any matting or artificial filming.

In the Washington and Lincoln bays at the west end of the nave the abstract designs of rich color are related to the lives of these great leaders. A new nation in the image of a growing green tree is suggested in the Washington bay, whereas the agony of our nation's Civil War is recalled in the Lincoln bay. Small windows high in the east walls of these bays relate to Martha Washington and Lincoln's mother and stepmother.

At north and south nave aisle level the designs of the windows suggest the upbuilding of the Body of Christ in the course of Christian history. Glass of the south aisle depicts artists, artisans, musicians, craftsmen, architects and scientists who through their chosen media have illuminated some of the ways and nature of God. Openings on the north side at this level depict Christian kings, statesmen, political leaders and philosophers who have worked through the political and governmental framework to express their faith. The figures in these designs have more natural flesh tones in the faces and hands and contain a rich variety of designs, having been created by eight different artists.

One window in this collection, the Space Window in the south aisle, is quite different from all other windows in the cathedral. In all cathedral windows, as in the best thirteenth century glass, there is little or no perception of depth. The glass is architectural, part of the walls and separating the interior from the exterior. The action is between the window opening mullions, or jambs. But in the space window the perception is different. The action is beyond the mullions, as if the viewer were looking at the cosmos and beyond at the heavenly bodies. The glass commemorates man's first landing on the moon.

Low outer aisle bay windows in the nave depart from the plan in not having a predetermined unity. Each window relates only to the theme of that memorial bay and takes its inspiration from some aspect of the person memorialized. Hence, the windows have a wide diversity of subjects—historical, biblical, secular and theological. Most of this glass is free of filming and very luminous in color.

The cathedral was built east to west, thus the glass of the south transept represents an earlier era in stained-glass making except for the six clerestory windows that are contemporary with the nave clerestory windows. The two west aisle windows around the baptismal font illustrate the history and theology of the sacrament of Baptism. Higher in this west aisle wall is a small window depicting the healing grace of Christ, suggested in the raising of Jairus' daughter from the dead. Through baptism we are reborn and through Christ's redemptive action in our lives we can be healed and freed from sin.

High in this transept the twelve-petaled rose window expresses the climax of the clerestory window themes, depicting the great streams of the Christian faith as they will culminate in the church triumphant. God the father is the central figure. Beneath the rose the three twin-lanceted windows feature six of the apostles, including Thomas who has a strange green beard! On the east side of this transept clerestory are rendered the early church at Jerusalem, the Roman Catholic and the Orthodox streams of Christianity. On the west are the Anglican stream, the Reformation movement and the ecumenical movement of the twentieth century—tormented as it has been by pride and separation.

In the dramatic War Memorial Chapel of this transept, the imagery denotes sacrifice and the struggle for human freedom. Vignettes at the bottom of each lancet portray scenes from contemporary history in World War II. Figures in these chapel windows range from Richard the Lion Hearted to the four chaplains who laid down their lives for their friends. These windows are excellent examples of the skillful use of silver-white beading and fillet lines in classical Gothic-style glass.

Jesus' miracles are recounted in quite detailed style in the glass of St. John's Chapel. These medallion designs feature a host of small figures. The windows include a substantial amount of green/white glass and much detail reminiscent of the English glass in Bethlehem Chapel. As a general rule, the lower and nearer the window to eye level the more detail the artist is permitted to include in the design. This amount of detailing diminishes as the windows are placed higher in the walls.

In the apse the five windows facing west and surrounding the sanctuary and high altar show major events in the life of Christ. From left to right, the first window on the north side treats in most loving fashion the childhood of Jesus; this is followed by the Crucifixion; Christ ruling in majesty; the Resurrection; and to the far south side, the Transfiguration.

On the north and south sides of the sanctuary between apse and choir are the very tall Te Deum windows packed with detail and figures. In nearly every respect they fail to fulfill the Building Committee's mandates for good stained glass and will probably be replaced later.

The choir clerestory windows recall angelic appearances in the Bible. On the north are the angels of the Old Testament and on the south, those of the New Testament. In religious symbolism it is traditional for old Testament themes to be on the north side and New Testament on the south. This is a symbolic way of saying that the coming of Christ brought light to the world. Artists are aware of the enormous difference in the light conditions between the north, or dark, side of the cathedral and the south, or sun, side.

In the Chapel of the Holy Spirit the single window tells the story of the woman of Samaria when she offers Jesus water at the well. At first thought this may seem a strange story for this chapel, but the same passage in John's gospel records that God is a spirit and those that worship him must worship him in truth and spirit.

In the north transept rose, the first rose installed in the cathedral, the text enunciated in the biblical Last Judgment is depicted. The multiple stone openings incorporate a vast number of diminutive figures nearly unreadable from the floor of the cathedral. The three windows beneath it feature twelve Old and New Testament persons who foretold the Last Judgment. In addition to being north windows—on the dark side—these windows also incorporate heavy filming typical of an earlier style of window making.

The six clerestory windows of this transept have no iconographic relationship to its rose. However, they and the other windows of this transept have a strong patriotic flavor. This is expressed by portrayal of many national leaders and statesmen. The east clerestory glass is devoted to the themes of education, law and healing. The west side denotes leaders of South America and Canada, along with an English window devoted to the Anglican Book of Common Prayer. At lower levels the windows feature Old Testament figures such as Moses, Deborah, Barak and Daniel. Americans Thomas Jefferson and James Madison are included. Here also Florence Nightingale is featured in a full window. The twin openings of the parclose stairway leading to the crypt chapels from this transept have interesting representations of truth and falsehood.

If the changing iconographic pattern in the growth of the cathedral was true in the story-telling, the change in design styles was even more exciting. These are outlined by artist Rowan LeCompte in the next chapter.

The viewer should be aware that there are dozens of splendid small single lancet windows tucked away in turret stairs and far corners of this great structure. Each one carries symbols and a message of its own, there being no predetermined themes for these intimate examples of the glass designer's art.

RICHARD T. FELLER
Canon Clerk of the Works

A lancet of the Statesmen window in the north transept shows Thomas Jefferson

history and techniques

"Only works of art done by passionate, burning love bear the mark of validity in buildings of dignity . . ." Ervin Bossanyi

Stained glass, an ancient art, flourished in the Middle Ages but fell into decline in the Renaissance and remained insignificant until its revival in the early nineteenth century. Thereafter it was, and is, employed on a large scale in America and Europe, often in uninspired Gothic imitations and other conventional and commercial forms. But during its revival, and since, an increasing number of real artists in stained glass have appeared; their varied contributions to its development as a vital art make a fascinating continuing story.

That art is as crowded with difficulties as it is with delights. Those who would practise it creditably must learn drawing, composition, form, color—the usual disciplines of painters; then the essential techniques of window structure and fabrication; then a further and more difficult subtlety, the most telling ways of "painting" with light, articulating light. Intermingled notes of colored light can so easily be inharmonious, harsh or dull, disorganized, flat or out of control. But they are called to sing. The great windows do sing.

The parallels to music are many. Like song, stained glass can communicate ideas, can teach. But, like music, its core is aesthetic and emotional. Installed in buildings where it can fulfill—or frustrate—a powerful architectural role in admitting and tempering the light, its primary purposes are more ethereal: It can stimulate the imagination; like music it can lift the heart; it can enchant.

Washington Cathedral's stained glass program began shortly before 1912 along respectable and very conventional lines, continuing in neo-Gothic traditions until 1953 when Evie Hone's more urbane and adventurous window arrived from Dublin. Since then, in very lively progress, artists native to eight countries have carried out commissions which have enhanced the cathedral with their remarkable, individual visions of what is beautiful and appropriate for it. In large measure their works have been mutually sympathetic, yet each is unique, seeking to enrich the great building not by lifelessly imitating medieval styles or "modern" fashions, but by an imaginative search for scale, forms and rhythms appropriate to the architecture and to each window's subject and situation.

This approach, pairing the breadth of sensitivity and imagination absolutely

11

Rowan LeCompte (left) prepares to cut a small piece of glass to fit the paper pattern. Master craftsman Dieter Goldkuhle (right) will cut and trim the glass to fit exactly.

indispensable in the cathedral's administrators with the artist's creative talent and longed-for inspiration, offers the best, perhaps the only, possibility that the glass will be living art. That it should be vividly alive is the more important because of the cool elegance of the cathedral's architecture; if its windows can blaze with spirt and ardor, this church will become a great stone lantern, lifting up people's hearts by its massive, awesome grace, warming them in its vital light.

What Stained Glass Is

A stained glass window is seldom "stained" and is really a kind of translucent mosaic in which pieces of glass, colored when sand and mineral oxides are melted together in a furnace, are assembled to create a pattern of light. The glasses can be of many kinds, transparent, cloudy, colorless or strongly colored, and are fitted and bound together in grooved strips of lead, though other materials can be used also. Glass can be painted with various mineral pigments fired-in to be permanent, but because the most intense effects of color are seen in glass colored in its original molten state, painting is generally confined to black mineral pigment which can be applied as inky line or grayish cloudy film.

Stained glass windows are conveniently made only in smallish sections, so large windows must be composed of many such panels assembled in place and

High above the west end of the nave, Dieter Goldkuhle fits a completed panel into a stone groove in a section of a window. The glass pieces have been fitted into strips of grooved lead which have in turn been soldered together on both sides of the panel.

supported and braced by metal bars anchored to the frame. In spite of its apparent fragility, leaded stained glass can, when well made, last many centuries. Some windows from the 12th, 13th and 14th centuries have survived into modern times in their original leading, and medieval windows, of which a surprising number yet remain, would be far more numerous today if thousands had not been deliberately destroyed in wars of religion, waves of fanatical vandalism and the 18th century's distaste for old-fashioned "gothick."

History and Technique

Glass and the procedures for coloring it with metallic oxides have been known for thousands of years, but it was only at the time of Christ that glassblowing was discovered, and, with it, techniques for producing large pieces of workably thin transparent glass. During the so-called Dark Ages some now unknown inventor, perhaps inspired by the golden wires that separate segments of color in Byzantine enamels, conceived of assembling pieces of colored glass by means of grooved strips of metal; lead is supremely useful for that purpose because it is cheap, malleable and waterproof. But lead is soft and heavy, so, in order not to sag and bulge, panels of leaded glass need to be well braced and stiffened by iron or bronze bars attached to the surface; like the heavier structural bars that

13

LeCompte applies lines, patterns and hatchings of black paint to colored glass which has been cut and mounted temporarily on plate glass windows so that light can come through. Later the glass is fired in an electric kiln.

separate and support each panel, such bars, seen against the light as black lines, are never visually objectionable when planned as part of a window's design.

Washington Cathedral's windows are all fabricated in the classical technique which was followed throughout the Middle Ages. It requires, first, the artist's design, then the enlargement of that design to full size. This is called the cartoon, and from it paper patterns are made showing the exact shape of each piece of glass. Pieces of colored glass are then selected and cut from small handblown sheets to match the patterns. Any glasses to receive painting are then painted, then fired to their melting point, 1200 degrees F., for the paint to

14

be permanently fused. The finished pieces are then assembled in machined
strips of tough lead alloy which resemble small I-beams; the leads' intersections
are soldered on both faces, weather-proof cement is squeezed into all crevices,
and the completed panels are ready for assembling with their necessary rein-
forcing bars in the cathedral walls.

The origins of stained glass are obscure. It may well have been a Byzantine
invention, but in any case was being practised as a church art in Western Europe
by the 10th century and perhaps long before. Once the technique for assembling
many bits of glass to form compositions had been worked out, and such
compositions were studied against light — mounted, that is, in window openings
so as to shine with the brilliant light of the sky into a relatively dim interior — it
was understood that a wholly new and astonishing invention was at hand, one in
which light and the controlled play of light were of unique and supreme impor-
tance. Because windows against the sky blaze with a literally unearthly light,
combinations of colored glasses set there can glow and change with every
passing cloud, sparkling with an eloquence unequalled in any other art. Only

Exterior view of the Creation (West) Rose

fireworks, glorious and fugitive, share the intensities of light available to stained glass; painting, colored sculpture, even sparkling glass mosaics and jewels are seen by reflected light, and look subdued by comparison. However, the fiercely radiant colors of glass powerfully affect each other, and can more easily become garish and mutually antagonistic than harmonious.

Medieval Brillance

A long period of observation and development must have followed the earliest essays in the new art and many fascinating works must have perished, because the oldest windows still extant, at Augsburg Cathedral, which date from the 11th century, are of striking artistic quality; a few older works are known only as fragments. But a number of windows from the 12th century still grace the interiors for which they were made; their quality is marvelous. In their ravishing harmony of color, composition and scale, their graphic power, their sparkle and glow, they reveal an understanding of the effects of color in light and distance, together with a mastery of stained glass as a luminous architectural art, which has never been surpassed. Major examples of that exquisite art of the 12th century can be seen at Poitiers, Chartres, Strasbourg and Canterbury; battered by time and mischance, they are still wonderfully beautiful and moving.

In the vast wave of church-building in the "French Style" or New Style" that followed the invention of Gothic at St. Denis about 1140, innumerable windows were commissioned and made, and stained glass became the crowning architectural art of the age. Medieval windows are always interesting, but are by no means always successful in their handling of the supreme problem: the organization and expressive control of form and color in light at varying distances. These are subtle difficulties that naturally were better mastered by some artists than by others.

A Fading Light

In the late Middle Ages and Renaissance, glass lost its character as an art of architectural appropriateness. The naturalistic approach of the easel painter and muralist was all in vogue, and the efforts of window makers to work along such lines, following pictorial principles rather than those of decorative design, resulted in a disastrous decline of essential stained-glass-window qualities. Stained glass became a "lost art," not because its physical techniques were ever entirely forgotten, but because its right principles were.

A Light Eclipsed

In the United States, in the last third of the nineteenth century, a new kind of seductively smooth pictorial window was developed by John LaFarge and amplified by Louis C. Tiffany. Using multiple layers of a cloudy colored glass of their own invention, with almost no painting, they achieved soft effects of extreme naturalism, a softness jarred by the visually intrusive black lines of structural bars and leads necessary for the construction of their windows. To such windows other objections could be found also. They were usually excessively narrative or "literary" and often sentimentally saccharine; because their cloudy glass was the opposite of clear and sparkling, they made interiors dull and static; by their pictorialism they changed the window's vital role as an architecturally decorative source of light to that of the window as a narrative part of the wall, heavy and relatively unluminous. It can reasonably be argued that Louis Tiffany took stained glass an unprecedented distance in a wrong direction.

The chief thing that led Tiffany and other picture-window makers astray was the false idea that stained glass should be—or even can be—pictorially "realistic." Any art made of rough or glittering or other self-assertive materials—such as

Early windows (around 1100) in Augsburg, Germany, depict Daniel and David

mosaic, stained glass, wrought iron, welded sculpture—can never attempt the illusion of naturalism without looking false and ridiculous. A strong material needs to be seen as *itself,* hence must be allowed due emphasis in works designed to show its character to sympathetic advantage.

A Light Rekindled

Before 1855 a study of the rich handblown glass in medieval windows by Charles Winston in England had enabled him and other enthusiastic antiquarians to make new colored glasses of comparable beauty. Such handmade glass, like that of the early Middle Ages—and like that used since in the windows of Washington Cathedral—has the qualities and variations essential to the liveliest and most beautiful effects of light. It is transparent and irregular, often bubbly, always of varying thickness and texture, with a shimmering liquid beauty, exciting and mysterious. It has come to be called "antique" glass because of its resemblance to the ancient material, in contrast to less interesting machine-made glasses and the milky "opalescent" glass developed by LaFarge and Tiffany. Rumors still persist that certain medieval colors are unreproducible, that "secrets" have been lost. Untrue. Every medieval color has been achieved again in the past century, plus many colors and textures unknown to the ancients.

Early in the Gothic Revival, which was part of the nineteenth century's Romantic movement, attention began to be paid to medieval windows and to the many reasons for their beauty. These were scrutinized, and research published, by discerning and influential scholars like E. Viollet-le-Duc. Expanded interest in England and France initially produced many tame imitation-medieval windows like those in the cathedrals of Peterborough and Périgueux, but more personal and meaningful windows soon began to be seen in England when D. G. Rossetti, William Morris and others similarly gifted and sincere took up stained glass with serious artistic purpose. By 1900 much interesting new work had been done by individual artists like Christopher Whall and Edward Burne-Jones in Europe, none so fine as the great medieval windows, but much of it worthy of very serious consideration and admiration.

But, long before, large stained glass *firms* had sprung up, employing many designers and huge staffs; their productive capacity was immense. Big English and German companies made windows totalling many thousands of square yards for churches all over the world. Standardized English Victorian saints, glassy pale, gazed blandly at their exotic settings from Bombay to Manitoba. Not all these carefully polished works were artistically insignificant, though certainly most were; those windows principally told stories in a very usual and mildly inoffensive way, and were "proper" and soothing rather than in the least inspired. Most imitated some aspects of medieval style, but without strength or conviction. None sang as had the harmonious jewels of the mighty 12th century.

Washington Cathedral and Neo-Gothic Windows

Washington Cathedral's first stained glass windows, those of the Bethlehem Chapel, were commissioned in 1912 from such a firm, the large and prestigious

one of Kempe and Company in London. The actual designer of the windows, John Lisle, has only recently been generally recognized.

In the interval between the Bethlehem Chapel windows and the commissioning of the first glass in 1928 for the newly rising walls of the cathedral choir, important developments took place in stained glass in this country and Europe. Johan Thorn-Prikker and Josef Albers were among the progressive artists designing new glass in a vigorous modern style in Germany, and, in Ireland, Harry Clarke, an artist of genius, had before 1920 achieved at Cork perhaps the most intense expression of form, color and personality that had been combined in glass since the Middle Ages. In Boston, Harry Eldredge Goodhue (d. 1918) became the American pioneer of transparent, formally designed stained glass, as opposed to the opalescent picture-window then all the rage. Also in Boston was Ralph Adams Cram, the eloquent and influential American medievalist-architect. He energetically championed a number of new American glass artists who, like Harry Goodhue, tended (especially before 1930) to be romantics, and whose enthusiasm for ancient windows led them along eclectic and picturesque paths. Their growing number came to include William Willet, Henry Wynd Young, Nicola D'Ascenzo, J. Gordon Guthrie, G. Owen Bonawit, Ernest Lakeman, Wilbur Herbert Burnham and Joseph G. Reynolds. The last two men were active at Washington Cathedral from 1938 until 1963; many of Mr. Reynolds's windows were designed by N. A. Setti, who later became an independent cathedral artist.

But of all these artists, some of whom acquired large staffs, some of whom worked almost alone, by far the best known and most influential was Charles J. Connick.* His masterpiece, the choir glass at Princeton, remains an undiscovered national treasure. The most gifted of all those men was certainly Harry Goodhue's son, Wright Goodhue. His brief career began at 19 years of age; the next year, 1925, he designed his exquisite Pre-Raphaelite windows at Mercersburg. He died in 1931, the same year as his distinguished Irish counterpart, Harry Clarke. In Goodhue's most beautiful work, ancient forms glow with the vivid aura of his mysterious personality.

In 1928 Washington Cathedral, with its choir and north transept under construction, began the work of its major windows under the guidance of Lawrence B. Saint, one of the artists who had contributed to the Swedenborgian cathedral at Bryn Athyn, Pennsylvania, and who was known as the very able illustrator of Hugh Arnold's book, "Stained Glass of the Middle Ages in England and France." Mr. Saint was commissioned to design and make a continuing series of windows for Washington Cathedral, using entirely the beautiful medieval-type glass that he and his staff hoped to produce. After many trials and errors, of which he has left a valuable and amusing technical description, Mr. Saint and his assistants did indeed create with brilliant success a variety of glasses extremely close in color and quality to the medieval palette. He then designed and made the seven windows in the Chapels of St. Mary and

---

*Charles J. Connick (1875-1945) writer, artist and lecturer, a friend of poetry and scholarship

St. John, the Moses and the Barak windows in the north transept, the north rose window and the three windows beneath, and his masterpiece, the two windows on the parclose stairway. Mr. Saint's work reflects his fervor of evangelical belief. His designs drew strength from the sincerity of his convictions.

Also executed at Lawrence Saint's Huntingdon Valley studio in 1934 were the first three windows for the choir clerestory, which had been designed by Earl Edward Sanborn (1890-1937), of Annisquam, Massachusetts. Mr. Sanborn, a meticulous artist of gentle and winning civility—whose best work is in another Frohman, Robb and Little building, the chapel of Trinity College, Hartford—designed and made in his own studio the pair of 65-foot windows (Te Deum) that the architects had intended to light the area of the cathedral's high altar.

Ancient and Neo-Gothic Glasspainting

Painting in medieval windows was largely limited to the black lines that showed faces, hands and folds of garments, and also formed the decorative patterns like beading that subdued excessive brightness and added delicacy of sparkling detail. Filming was minimal, just a pale, partial modelling on figures which was intended to increase legibility. Backgrounds, except for those few patterned all over with a dark floral or geometric pattern, were unpainted, and blazed away in clear red or blue splendor.

But medieval windows are mostly so dulled and weatherworn today that it is hard to imagine their original, extreme transparency and brilliance "when the cathedrals were white." Famous windows like the many still uncleaned in the nave at Chartres, darkly haunting in their glowing obscurity, and profoundly impressive, are nevertheless radically different from the tapestries of dancing light they were when installed in the 13th century. The glass of course accumulates dirt, but that is fairly easily cleaned away; far more serious is the actual loss of the glassy surface, the scaling and pitting that at once thin and blacken soft ancient glass, showing on the outside not its original dark polish but a surface as pale and roughened as the surrounding stone walls. Not only have many medieval windows all but ceased to admit light to their interiors, not only has their color been sadly darkened and its cheerful liveliness and balance obscured, but another related loss has diminished their original effect: being no longer transparent, they no longer can admit the floods of colored sunshine that once washed over cathedral floors and walls on bright days. Imagine the radiance of Chartres in the 13th century: the pale interior walls interrupted everywhere by great windows which sparkle with thousands of pieces of white and colored glass, each window catching the sun also projecting a blurry, bright image of its colored pattern onto the floor or wall or column opposite. No wonder that medieval scholars and churchmen considered light the supreme symbol of God, and the transfigured light in their cathedrals as a token of Heaven made available to human understanding.

But time, which overtakes all human works, has subdued that light. Even three centuries ago Milton spoke of church windows "casting a dim religious light;" in the 13th century it would have been an overwhelming religious light!

Detail of Angels of Deliverance window in north choir clerestory

Nevertheless, in the dusky, time-stained, shadowy look of ancient glass many 20th century glass artists have taken much pleasure, even to the extent of filming, smudging and antiquing their own new work—with dark paint fired in to be permanent. The effects are several: windows can instantly be made mellow, easy on the eyes, mysterious; the animation of darting colored light is stilled, and easily controlled; small patterns gain in legibility; a dazzling exposure can be subdued. But this practice of filming has decidedly negative aspects: the window's liveliness is reduced; its colors to some extent are muddied; its clean glassy textures disappear; it admits less light, sometimes almost none, and its capacity for projecting colored sunbeams is stifled.

Lawrence Saint, like most of his contemporaries, was fascinated by the shadows of decay on ancient glass and was convinced they increased its beauty. Therefore all his windows in Washington Cathedral, made of spectacular glass which had been achieved at such cost, are filmed on their inside surfaces and spattered on the outside with black specks that resemble pitting. The colors are flattened and dulled, the liquid textures clouded over.

E. E. Sanborn's tall apse windows are even more heavily filmed; the flood of light expected from them has to be supplied instead by floodlights mounted in their reveals.

But, contrary to medieval practice and regardless of its disadvantages, all the large windows installed in Washington Cathedral until 1962 continued to be clouded over with such a permanent film of obscuring paint.

The very first glass in the building to be free of all filming was the small lancet (1951) by G. Robert Lewis in the Mellon Bay. Nevertheless, for some years the installation of filmed-down major windows, generally designed with similarly quiet decorous conservatism, continued. The north transept thus lost most of the light which had come in earlier through temporary glass in its clerestory.

Washington Cathedral's New Glass

But with the advent of the south transept window (1953) by the famous Irish artist Evie Hone, whose muted color is in contrast to her free drawing and contained rhythms of her masterly composition, the cathedral's glass began to move toward freer kinds of design and cleaner, brighter effects of light. Rowan and Irene LeCompte's Humanitarian windows (1955 and 1956), packed with detail and restrained emotion, were entirely transparent, as was their Nativity window (1960) in the choir clerestory, the first unfilmed window of major size in the building.

The new glass of the nave is richly varied and reasonably luminous and unified, representing as it does the work of more than ten different personalities. It includes in the Wilson Bay the masterpiece of Ervin Bossanyi, an intensely personal and emotional artist, whose pantheist sympathies were touched by German Expressionism, the art of the East and his country childhood in Hungary. All of Bossanyi's windows in the nave aisles come from his heart, his candor, confidence and passionate innocence.

Rowan LeCompte's west rose window (1973-76) is unique in the extent of time and freedom granted the artist and his craftsman-collaborator, Dieter Goldkuhle, and also in its extensive combination of antique glass, painted with abstract patterns, prisms and thick jewel-like nuggets of chipped colored glass.

The west nave contains two groups of intense and remarkable windows by the very distinguished German artist, Hans Kaiser (1913-1982). Their glowing clouds of color, broken into rich granulation by mazes of leadlines, are scenes from a master's spiritual journey, and are his homage to the burning mysteries at the heart of his medium and its gemmed lights and shadows.

Other memorable glass in the west nave includes the luminous and varied work of Robert Pinart. His vivid windows for the Washington and Lincoln bays symbolize poignant episodes in America's past, and demonstrate the communicative power of abstract pattern and color alone.

Strikingly different from those two windows are his many designs without color that quietly enrich the narthex and other nearby walls. The eye passes easily through their beautiful handmade white glass to see the architecture as through a curtain of clear water.

The nave clerestory, the last group of major windows to be undertaken, will, it is hoped, bring into balance when completed intensities of expression and diversity within a great overall unity. Because there will be many different subjects, many moods will be explored, from Abraham's fatherly anguish to the rapture of Job's vision of redemption. There will be many kinds of pattern, many differing rhythms, many varieties and combinations of color. May all the windows ultimately work together to achieve a great visual music that will sing harmoniously with the architecture, that will truly lift the heart, that will in every moment of daylight offer up its radiant prayer of passionate praise and gratitude.

Rowan LeCompte

Fisher of Men (St Peter) in the north nave cleresto

Rowan LeCompte's masterpiece, the great west rose, is the first window described in this walking tour of the stained glass of Washington Cathedral. It is followed by the Churchill window in the St. Paul tower porch (south) and the Dickinson window in the St. Peter tower porch (north).

Between the narthex, the porches and the nave of the cathedral are the leaded, clear windows designed by Robert Pinart. Made of hand-blown, textured "Dresden" glass, these windows are part of what the artist describes as "a happy marriage" with the carved stone seen through them. Note the wider black lines in the glass. These are narrow traceries of black glass leaded to the "white" glass.

After you have entered the main body of the cathedral through the west doors turn to the right towards the Washington Bay. The highest window directly above the bay is the "Ruth" window on the extreme west end of the south clerestory. This is where to begin.

The nave windows are numbered in sequence to enable the visitor to view them at a distance, looking up to the highest level (clerestory) and descending to the middle row (nave aisle) and finally to the lowest level (nave outer aisle).

A self-guided tour of the main floor takes the visitor from the west end, along the south side proceeding in a counter-clockwise direction, eventually returning to the starting point.

1 THE CREATION ROSE (1976)
Theme: The Creation
Memorials: William Douglas Sloane and Malcolm Douglas Sloane
Artist: Rowan LeCompte

The creation theme for the west rose was adopted by the Cathedral Chapter in 1935. It is a ten petal rose. A rose window is so subdivided by masonry that it becomes *all* tracery. There is no space for figures which would be large enough to be seen from the nave floor. Artist Rowan LeCompte chose to make the window in pure color and free form.

The artist takes his cue from the Book of Genesis, "and the earth was without form and void and darkness was upon the face of the deep" . . . "and God said, Let there be light."

The center of the window has deep mysterious colors with a single piece of burning white glass at its very core. From this center the light radiates outward and the colors of the window turn brighter as the eye moves toward the outer petals. While the predominant color is blue, it has large areas of fall colors.

The window was fabricated by LeCompte in collaboration with Dieter Goldkuhle.

2 THE LAND IS BRIGHT (1974)
Memorial: Winston Churchill
Artist: John Piper

Located in the south gallery of the porch is the three lancet abstract stained glass window designed by the English artist, John Piper, and fabricated by his associate Patrick Reyntiens. The artist's inspiration for the design was based on the following verse from a poem by Arthur Hugh Clough and quoted by Sir Winston Churchill in his world broadcast of April 27, 1941:
"And not by eastern windows only,
when daylight comes, comes in the light;
in front the sun climbs slow, how slowly!
But westward, look the land is bright."

3 THE DICKINSON WINDOW (1976)
In honor and gratitude for the Fairleigh Dickinson family
Artist: Hans Kaiser

The abstract design suggests the blessing of God's healing through herbs and medicines of the earth. The deeper tones stand for pain and mystery; the lighter colors represent hope and God's healing power.

As the west rose window attests to the divine origin of all life, the remainder of the cathedral interior offers a perception of God's covenant with man. . . . The nave clerestory window themes are taken from the Old Testament and offer clues to God's presence in aiding the human spirit as it moves from mortality to eternity.

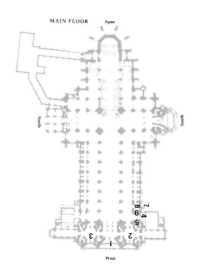

MAIN FLOOR Apse

North

South

West

4 RUTH AND NAOMI (1977)
Memorial: Olive Warfield King
Artist: Rowan LeCompte

The westernmost south clerestory window illustrates the earth as shelter and features figures from the Book of Ruth. The dominant figure is Ruth, in the left center lancet . . . to the viewer's right is portrayed Naomi, the cared-for dependent as indicated by her leaning posture. With her left hand she is beckoning Ruth toward Boaz. Ruth is shown carrying sheaves of wheat which she has harvested from the fields of Boaz.

In the right-hand lancet is portrayed Boaz cheerfully welcoming a new life with Ruth. The left outer lancet without a human figure features a large olive tree symbolizing the fruitful earth as God's gift to man. The multifoil at the top of the tracery shows a boy gardening in the fruitful earth. This is Obed, child of the union of Ruth and Boaz.

The window was fabricated by the Greenland Studio, New York.

5 THE FOUNDING OF A NEW NATION (1976)
Memorial: Alexander C. and Priscilla Liggett
Artist: Robert Pinart

The abstract design of the window reflects the search for freedom which led to the founding of the United States. The dark colors below suggest tyranny and oppression; the reds indicate the bloodshed in the struggle for nationhood; the greens remind us of the country's growth and the upper blues of open space.

The grey glass might convey the idea of smoke from Indian campfires or the various times of strife the nation has endured. In the tracery glass at the top are the red, white and blue of the flag.

The windows in the Washington Bay were fabricated by Dieter Goldkuhle.

6 MARTHA WASHINGTON (1978)
Memorial: Minnie Catherine Loud
Artist: Brenda Belfield

Martha Washington and the home she made at Mount Vernon for George Washington were a great source of strength to the first President. The window represents the activities and homelife of the Washington family: a shell taken from a motif on dining room chairs, colonial quilt patterns, a dove from a Mount Vernon weathervane, holly berries and dogwood from the garden, the stars of the Washington coat of arms and the pineapple of hospitality.

7 ABRAHAM AND ISAAC—THE SACRIFICE (1979)
Memorial: Hugh Leander and Mary Trumbull Adams; John Hillary and Mary Payne Trumbull
Artist: Rowan LeCompte

Two major events in the life of Abraham, the birth of Isaac to Sarah, and God's command that Abraham take Isaac to become a human sacrifice, are the focal points of the iconography. The dominant figure is Abraham, his twisted feet clutching the rocky mountainside as he writhes in agony, preparing to obey God's awful command to sacrifice his son Isaac. The color around Abraham suggests the intense heat of a sacrificial fire, though no flames are to be seen. Other figures in the window include the aged Sarah and the infant Isaac, the slave Hagar and her son Ishmael, and the ram caught by his horns in a thicket of brush.

The window was fabricated in the Greenland Studio, New York.

8 HEALING ARTS (1979)
Memorial: Charles Frederic Wilson
Artist: Charles Z. Lawrence

The Healing Arts window gives symbolic recognition to those in the field of medical technology and to those who have initiated significant discoveries in the fight against disease of mind and body.

The major subject of the center lancet is a knight hospitaler of the Order of Hospitalers of St. John of Jerusalem, the most important of the military orders organized before the Crusades.

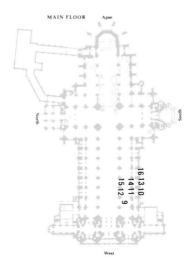

MAIN FLOOR Apse

North

South

West

In the predella are pioneers of medical research and discovery: Sir William Harvey, an Anglican born in 1578, was personal physician to King Charles I and is credited with the discovery of the circulation of the blood; Joseph Lister, born 1812, served as an English surgeon attached to Edinburgh infirmary and discovered the use of antiseptic; Walter Reed, the American who headed the Yellow Fever Commission to Cuba in 1900, proved that Yellow Fever, caused by mosquitoes, was not contagious.

The right lancet directs attention to mental health, the major figure being Christ healing the Gerasene demoniac. The predella suggests Dr. Charles F. Menninger and his sons, Drs. Karl and William Menninger, of the Menninger Foundation, Topeka, Kansas, pioneers in American psychiatric treatment and care.

The dominant figure of the left lancet is the prophet Elisha healing the Syrian commander Naaman of leprosy. The predella recalls two pioneers in medical research: Marie Curie, who with her husband, Pierre, isolated radium; and Wilhelm Roentgen, who in his Bavarian laboratory in 1895 discovered the X-ray.

The window was fabricated in the Willet Stained Glass Studios, Philadelphia, Pennsylvania.

9 RELIGIOUS FREEDOM IN MARYLAND (1972)
Memorials: Anna Campbell Ellicott, Charlotte Campbell Nelson, Ella Campbell Smythe
Artist: Rowan LeCompte

Figures in Maryland's history depicted in this window are: in the left lancet, Francis Asbury, the first Methodist bishop consecrated in America, and George Fox, founder of the Society of Friends. The right lancet shows the first Roman Catholic bishop in America, John Carroll, with a sketch of Georgetown University, which he founded. Below Bishop Carroll is a depiction of the first Roman Catholic mass celebrated in America and its celebrant, Father Andrew White SJ.

In the center lancet is the first Episcopal bishop consecrated in America, Thomas John Claggett. The eary explorer, Captain John Smith, is also shown. Below the lancets are flora and fauna characteristic of Maryland.

The window commemorates the Act of Toleration, passed by the Maryland General Assembly in 1649. This was the first instance where trinitarian Christians made legal their efforts to live together in harmony.

10 TIME AND HISTORY—JESSE, DAVID AND LINEAGE OF JESUS
Artist: Rowan LeCompte (commissioned)

11 POETS AND WRITERS (1973)
Memorials: Grace Barclay Adams Howard and Beale Richardson Howard
Artist: Rowan LeCompte

Three literary giants representative of three major streams of Christendom: Eastern Orthodoxy, Roman Catholicism and Protestantism are portrayed. In the left lancet, John Chrystostom, patriarch of Constantinople, appears; the center lancet is devoted to Dante Alighieri, author of *The Divine Comedy*. He looks up to Beatrice, who revealed paradise to him, and beyond her to the figure of Christ. John Milton dominates the right lancet, seen against the spire of St. Bride's Church, London. Below the figure of Milton is Satan, the protagonist in *Paradise Lost*.

Fabricator of the window was Dieter Goldkuhle.

12 EARLY MISSIONARIES OF THE NORTHWEST— "ODYSSEY OF THE SPIRIT" (1973)
Memorial: John Clifford Folger and Katherine Dulin Folger and children
Artist: Henry Lee Willet, Anthony Mako

The exploration of the northwest by Lewis and Clark, as a pictorial example of man's thrust to conquer the unknown, is the theme of these three lancets. Animals and flowers of the vast western states the explorers covered are depicted in each lancet. On the left are their large boat and canoes in which they left St. Louis in 1803. The center lancet depicts their meeting with the Sioux on the banks of the Missouri and the vast wilderness still lying before them. On the right can be seen the northwest timberland and above it the tree-covered promontory from which they first viewed the Pacific Ocean in 1805.

13 SUFFERING AND REDEMPTION—JOB
Memorial: Veterans of all wars
Artist: Rowan LeCompte (commissioned)

Founders window in south outer aisle of nave

14 ARCHITECTS AND SCULPTORS (1972)
Artist: Albert Birkle

The center lancet of this window is devoted to architects. King Solomon, builder of the great temple of Jerusalem, appears in the lower portion; Abbot Suger, builder of the Abbey of St. Denis and the innovator of Gothic architecture in the 12th century, and Sir Christopher Wren, architect of St. Paul's Cathedral, are also shown.

In the right and left lancets are depicted great works of sculpture and their creators from classical and contemporary times. The cinquefoil at the top shows the heavenly city of Jerusalem.

15 FOUNDERS—"MAN'S SEARCH FOR GOD" (1966)
Memorial: Charles Carroll Glover and Annie Cunningham Glover
Artist: Rowan and Irene LeCompte

These windows, with incidents taken from the Old and New Testaments, symbolize the spirit of the men who met in the home of Charles Carroll Glover on December 8, 1891, to plan the building of the cathedral.

The eastern lancet portrays the prophet Jeremiah, shackled in chains symbolic of his imprisonment. Beneath him is the city of Washington. In the upper portion the prophet is shown holding an evergreen tree, symbol of continuity and everlasting life. In the twin lancet St. Paul is seen as he preached on Mars Hill. In the quatrefoil above the two lancets is the Peace Cross, placed on Mount Saint Alban in 1898, marking the establishment of the cathedral church.

In the western lancets, the left one shows Jacob building an altar not of ordinary stones but with symbols of man's life and labor in the new world: a wigwam, an immigrant ship, a Colonial meeting house and a mill.

In the historic meeting in 1891, a group of men gathered at the Glover home to lay plans for the cathedral. In the lower portion of the right lancet, the artists have shown a small group sitting and talking. Next to them is a faithful reproduction of the Glover house. In the quatrefoil over the two lancets is the Jerusalem Cross, symbol of Washington Cathedral.

16 JEREMIAH (1981)
In thanksgiving: Mr and Mrs Henry H. Porter
Artist: Rowan LeCompte

The towering figure represents the major prophet Jeremiah, anguished, isolated, lonely and ignored. He preached repentance and the need of reform to a rich, indifferent society in a city beneath his feet. He prophesied that the temple would fall but that the people would survive. As a visionary Jeremiah saw that new life would come even as the people faced death.

In the left lancet is Baruch, a faithful scribe and disciple of Jeremiah. He read the word of Jeremiah to the worshippers in the hope that the grim prophecies would cause the people to repent.

The Old Testament prophet, Nahum in the right lancet, spoke out against Ninevah, capital of the Assyrian empire. Passionate in his vilification of the cruel power of Ninevah whose fall he predicted, Nahum is depicted with Assyrian rosettes and Ninevah's tumbling towers above him. The predellas contain symbols of the evils denounced by the prophets: manacles, money bags and a golden calf on an altar, a whip, daggers and chains. In the multifoil at the top of the window is a flowering almond tree referred to in one of Jeremiah's initial visions.

At midpoint in the nave, this window incorporates some of the

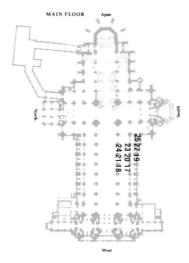

MAIN FLOOR Apse

North

South

West

finest individual pieces of glass in the cathedral. It was fabricated by Carl Edwards, of the Glasshouse, London.

17 SCIENTISTS AND TECHNICIANS [SPACE] (1973)
Artist: Rodney Winfield

Photographs taken during space travel provided the color inspiration for this window—dark spheres are punctuated by tiny white stars and, in the background, a thin white line suggests a spaceship trajectory. In the upper portion of the center lancet is a sliver of a lunar rock, presented to the cathedral by the astronauts of Apollo XI at the time of the window's dedication.

18 SPIRIT OF LAW (1959)
Memorial: Charles Warren
Artist: Napoleon Setti

A memorial to Charles Warren, distinguished lawyer and historian of the Supreme Court, the two windows in the Warren Bay portray the subject of law from a theological point of view, the meaning of law for the Christian. Since St. Paul had so much to say about law in his epistles, he is the central figure of the windows.

19 PSALMS (1982)
In honor of: Dean Emeritus Francis B. Sayre Jr.
Artist: Rowan LeCompte

Four major themes of the Psalms are represented (from right): *Lamentation*—a sorrowful man, beating his breast and heavy with chains, embodies grief, remorse, bitterness, fear of humiliation, the metaphorical chains shackling the human spirit. *Supplication*—a man rapt in prayer which rises from him in the form of an undulating flame. *Praise*—the rejoicing figure of a woman singing

"unto the Lord a new song." *Thanksgiving*—on the left, a jolly countryman expresses gratitude with a great scarf full of the fruits of the flowering earth. A cheerful band of musicians parades along the lower portion of all lancets.

The Sixty-Eighth Psalm tells us: "The singers went before, the players on instruments followed after; among them were the damsels playing with timbrels."

The rose at the top of the tracery shows a triple gateway, against a golden background, through which passes a radiant God, described in the Twenty-Fourth Psalm.

The window was fabricated by Dieter Goldkuhle under the direction of the artist.

20 ARTISANS AND CRAFTSMEN [LABOR] (1959)
Memorial: Samuel Gompers
Artist: Joseph G. Reynolds

The theme, "Housing of the Covenant," is a tribute to artisans and craftsmen who have given their utmost and the finest of their crafts to build a worthy tabernacle. In the left lancet Noah is shown building the ark. Above this the Ark of the Covenant is carried in procession, and finally, craftsmen are depicted building Washington Cathedral. The building of Solomon's Temple, the dedication of the temple and artisans embellishing Washington Cathedral are seen in the right lancet. In the central motif artists and craftsmen offer their works to Christ, the carpenter, depicted with a hand-saw in his left hand, his right hand raised in blessing. In the border are the thirty-six seals of the AFL-CIO unions.

21 WAR AND PEACE (1962)
Memorial: Woodrow Wilson
Artist: Ervin Bossanyi

The theme of Ervin Bossanyi's great lancet windows in the Wilson Bay is that of war and peace as these are perceived from within the Christian faith. Mr. Bossanyi was born in Hungary, lived later in Germany, but in 1934 fled from Leipzig to London. His greatest work grew out of the personal suffering and tragedy which he had seen, his windows became transformed into his prayer that mankind would turn to love and mutual understanding. While working on the windows, the artist wrote to Dean Sayre in April, 1955: "I would rather be without any work than to make windows that bear the mark of our unhappy age—that unhappy age your grandfather wanted mankind to be saved from."

22 THE FIRST COMMANDMENT—AMOS, HOSEA, MICAH
Memorial: General of the Army Douglas MacArthur
Artist: Rowan LeCompte
Fabricator: Dieter Goldkuhle

23 MUSICIANS AND COMPOSERS (1961)
Memorial: Henry A. Hurlbut Jr.
Artist: Napoleon Setti

The Virgin Mary, the predominant figure of the window, is depicted singing the first line of the Magnificat: "My soul doth magnify the Lord and my spirit hath rejoiced in God my Saviour." Hovering over her is a dove, symbol of the Holy Spirit, and beneath her feet are the shepherds listening to the heavenly host praising God. The predella of this center lancet portrays Deborah, Old Testament prophetess, under a palm tree singing: "Make a joyful noise unto the Lord." She carries cymbals, and at her side is the Star of David.

Praise to God the Father is summarized in the left lancet. In the top of the lancet a pair of hands is upraised in prayer with the word *Kyrie* inscribed beneath them. Beneath this is Johann Sebastian Bach, standing by the outline of a pipe organ, composing his famous B Minor Mass. In the predella of this lancet the contemporary composer, R. Vaughan Williams, conducts an orchestra in a church.

As the left lancet conveys praise to the Father, so the right lancet, with its symbolic lamb, conveys praise to God the Son. A bar of music showing the actual musical notation of the Agnus Dei is seen beneath the lamb. The central and largest figure of this lancet is that of John Merbecke, the well-known sixteenth century composer. To Merbecke's left is a group of black Americans who represent the rich contribution to religious compositions provided by their gospel music. St. Gregory, credited to be the father of Gregorian chant, is depicted in the predella of the lancet with a dove, symbolic of his divine inspiration.

24 LEE-JACKSON (1953)
Memorials: Robert E. Lee and Thomas J. (Stonewall) Jackson
Artist: Wilbur H. Burnham

The first window is devoted to General Lee in his role as engineer, military man and educator. The four medallions in the second window portray General Jackson as officer, teacher, in prayer on the battlefield, and "crossing over the river to rest in the shade of the trees." Worked into the design of the windows are flags associated with the two men. At the top is a symbolic representation of "the whole armor of God" suggesting the careers of these two Christian warriors.

25 ISAIAH (1981)
Memorial: Stuart Bradford and Florence Heaton Marshall
Artist: Rowan LeCompte

The dominant figure is Isaiah who experienced a powerful vision in the temple where an angel of the Lord reached down with a hot coal to touch his lips and cleanse him of sin, thus consecrating

The Law window in the north transept

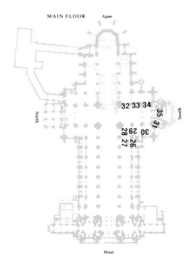

MAIN FLOOR   Apse

North   South

West

him as one of the great Old Testament prophets. Only after his purification could Isaiah prophesy the coming of Messiah. Micah, who also prophesied that a deliverer would come to establish a Messianic kingdom, is shown in the second lancet, gesturing down to the inevitable fall of an unrepentant Jerusalem. His raised arm points to a flowering tree to indicate the fruitful life of a humble, virtuous nation.

At the top, in the rose, a watchman, illustrating the text of Isaiah, "Watchman, what of the night?" peers anxiously from his tower for the coming of the savior and salvation. The rising sun is an Old Testament portent of the coming of Messiah.

Melville Greenland and artist Richard Avidon produced the window in the Greenland Studio, New York.

26 RELIGIOUS PAINTERS (1960)
Memorial: Francis Eudorah Pope
Artist: Joseph G. Reynolds

The Religious Painters window is based on the premise that all art is man's imitation of God's creation, the universe. The story told in the window begins with the artist's conception of the Creation in the center lancet. It continues with St. Luke who, according to Greek tradition, painted a picture of the Virgin. Accepted today as the patron saint of painters, he is shown sketching. Giotto, representing the creative medieval artists, holds the architectural plan for the Campanile which he designed and which still stands in Florence, Italy.

Depicted in other medallions are Albrecht Durer, German engraver and painter of the sixteenth century; a nameless illuminator representing those who embellished manuscripts and bibles of the Middle Ages; Fra Angelico whose religious frescoes adorn San Marco monastery in Florence, and Rembrandt, who with Durer represents the Protestant tradition in religious art.

27 PRESBYTERIAN HISTORY (1952)
Memorial: Andrew William Mellon
Artist: Robert Lewis

Three star-shaped medallions in the window show three major events in the history of the Presbyterian Church. At the top is the meeting in Philadelphia in 1706 to celebrate the organization of the Presbyterian Church in America; center, John Knox presents the Calvinistic Confession to the Scottish Parliament in 1560; bottom, John Calvin is depicted.

28 ST. PAUL WINDOW
Memorial: Edward Everett Loud
Artist: Rowan LeCompte

29 HEALING GRACE OF CHRIST (1953)
Memorial: Margot Garrett de Zuberbuhler
Artist: Evie Hone

The raising of Jairus' daughter is shown in the left lancet. In the right lancet can be seen the woman who touched Christ's hem and the healing of two blind men. This window is sometimes referred to as the "Irish window" in recognition of the nationality of the artist. Its installation marked the move towards freer design and cleaner, brighter effects of light in the cathedral's stained glass.

Baptistry

30 HISTORY OF BAPTISM (1954)
Memorial: Edward and Rahel O'Fon Davies
Artist: Wilbur H. Burnham

In the center lancet Christ commands his disciples, "Go ye into all the world and baptize." The group of seven who surround him are disciples drawn from ancient, medieval and modern times: St. Philip baptizing the Ethiopian eunuch, the baptism of Constantine, St. Francis Xavier baptizing in Japan, St. Columbia in Iona, and from the present day, Bishop Brent in the Philippines, a canon of Washington Cathedral baptizing an infant in Children's Chapel and the Reverend Thomas Mayhew on Martha's Vineyard with one of the first Indians baptized in this country. Worked into the border are traditional scallop shell and water, symbols of baptism, and also symbols of the Church of Wales, suggesting the Welsh ancestry of those commemorated.

31 THEOLOGY OF BAPTISM (1954)
Artist: Wilbur H. Burnham

The window in the south wall portrays the baptism of Christ. The seven medallions represent the principal parts of the baptismal service (1) "continue Christ's faithful soldier and servant"—St. Paul and the vision of the man from Macedonia; (2) "born anew of water and of the Holy Spirit"—Christ talking to Nicodemus by night; (3) "inheritor of the Kingdom of Heaven"—the stoning of St. Stephen; (4) "into the congregation of Christ's flock"—a group of disciples at Pentecost; (5) "mystical washing away of sin"—the woman taken in adultery; (6) "renounce the devil and all his works"—Christ's temptation and turning his back on the devil; (7) "believe in Jesus the Christ"—the confession of St. Peter in Christ as Messiah at Caesarea, Phillipi.

South Transept

East Clerestory

32 EARLY CHURCH AT JERUSALEM (1964)
Memorial: Henry St. George Tucker
Artist: Joseph G. Reynolds and Associates

The left lancet depicts St. Luke, the apostle and physician who travelled with Paul.

The center lancet shows the figure of St. James the Less holding a scroll suggesting the Epistle mentioned in Acts 15:30-31. The symbols of mortar and pestle denote St. Luke's devotion to medicine and the book stands for his Gospel.

At the top of this lancet, a group of heads in the cusps stands for the early apostles while the primitive Mediterranean ship suggests the travels they took to preach Christianity.

In the predella St. Philip is shown baptizing the Ethiopian. He is wearing typical Bedouin dress which is still worn today, in this case a blue striped coat with a yellow mantel and Arab head-dress. Cut into the background and border is the fuller's club with which he is said to have been martyred. Surrounding the head of James and continuing into the cusps a series of heads suggests the Council of Jerusalem. In the predella beneath the figure of James is St. Stephen, the first Christian martyr. Stephen kneels in the midst of a crowd of assassins armed with stones and staves.

In the right lancet is St. Mark, author of the second Gospel. The robes of St. Mark are patterned after the (Arab) dress of the day. The pen and book indicate authorship. In the predella is shown St. Peter baptizing the Roman Cornelius in his house at Caesarea.

A common Christian symbol found in the catacombs at Rome is the fish. It is also said to have been a password among the early followers of Christ. This symbol has been used in the borders of the three lancets.

In one of the quatrefoils in the tracery opening is the chrysanthemum, symbol of Japan, and here symbolic of Bishop Tucker's missionary activity in that country. In the second quatrefoil is the seal of the Diocese of Virginia, the bishop's home diocese.

33 ROMAN CATHOLIC STREAM OF CHRISTIANITY (1969)
Memorial: Mary Virginia Martin
Artist: Albert Birkle

The left (or northern) lancet is dominated by St. Thomas Aquinas (1226-1274) standing as the great codifier of law in the Roman church. Behind his head is a sunburst halo. He holds a quill, symbol of his writing. At the bottom of this lancet is St. Boniface, the great missioner to the Franks (680-755). He wears the mitre of the eighth century.

The center lancet shows Pope Gregory the Great, who lived from AD 540 to AD 604. The artist has robed him in pontifical clothing and a tiara, symbol of his office. In the predella beneath his figure is the dome of St. Peter's Basilica in Rome. Around it are a whole series of mitres representing Vatican councils.

The right hand lancet portrays St. Augustine of Hippo (AD 354 to AD 430). With him is the eagle which is his attribute. He is wearing a fourth century mitre and holds a fourth century form of crosier. In small vignette above the figure of St. Augustine is his mother, St. Monica. The predella recognizes the many great educators of the Roman church and portrays St. Ignatius Loyola (1491 to 1556). He is wearing the habit of a Jesuit, the order which he founded. Above him is the traditional IHS.

34 ORTHODOX STREAM OF CHRISTIANITY (1975)
Memorial: Athenagoras I
Artist: Albert Birkle

The three major figures of the Orthodox Church: The Virgin, Christ in Majesty and St. John the Baptist are featured. Colors reflect the mysticism and rich liturgical rites of the Orthodox Churches, and the style recalls the Byzantine heritage of their art. The predellas, from left to right, portray fathers of the early church: Chrysostom, Basil the Great, Demetrius, Gregory of Mazianzus and Athanasius.

35 THE CHURCH TRIUMPHANT (1962)
Memorial: Mary G. Kingsland
Artist: Joseph G. Reynolds and Wilbur H. Burnham

The south rose window shows the Church Triumphant, with its imagery taken from the Book of Revelation embodying St. John's vision of the throne of God in heaven. In the center medallion is seen God the Father, robed in a mantle of brilliant gold. In his left hand he holds the symbol, the Lamb of God. Around the throne are the winged heads of the four beasts, used as symbols of the four evangelists.

Twenty-four petal-shaped openings radiating from the six-lobed central form contain a rainbow around the throne of God. Next in sequence are the four and twenty Elders holding golden crowns. In the twelve six-foiled openings forming the perimeter of the rose

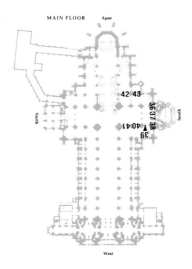

MAIN FLOOR   Apse

the twelve gates of heaven guarded by angels are suggested. Finally, biblical and saintly personages, who by their acts on earth achieved eternal glory in heaven, are depicted. Included are: the Archangel Gabriel, Saint Martin, the Archangel Michael, the Prodigal Son, St. Stephen. The window was completed in 1956. Dedication was in 1962.

36 THE APOSTLES (BARTHOLOMEW AND PHILIP) (1956)
Memorial: Mabel Stenwood Emery
Artists: Joseph G. Reynolds and Wilbur H. Burnham

37 THE APOSTLES (ANDREW AND JAMES) (1956)
Memorial: Lillian M. Oakley
Artists: Joseph G. Reynolds and Wilbur H. Burnham

38 THE APOSTLES (LUKE AND THOMAS) (1956)
Artists: Joseph G. Reynolds and Wilbur H. Burnham

West Clerestory

39 ANGLICAN STREAM OF CHRISTIANITY (1978)
Memorial: G. Lewis Jones
Artist: Eduard Renggli

The Anglican window depicts the Anglican stream which will one day merge with the five other great streams of Christendom. Symbolic figures include St. Augustine, reflecting the contribution of Roman missionaries to what was to become Anglicanism; Columba the monk, reflecting the Celtic contribution; and Archbishop Thomas Cranmer, creator of the Book of Common Prayer. Also shown are early American Episcopal churchman Phillips Brooks, English historian the Venerable Bede and symbols for Matthew, Mark, Luke and John, recalling the biblical foundation of the Anglican Church.

40 REFORMATION AND PROTESTANT STREAM OF CHRISTIANITY

41 COMING GREAT CHURCH (ECUMENICAL) (1973)
Memorial: Frances Berg Kemmer
Artist: Albert Birkle

The left lancet tells the Old Testament story of the Tower of Babel, the dark color palette of this lancet suggesting the dismay of division. The right lancet signifies newly baptized Christians eagerly awaiting the coming of the Holy Spirit through the laying on of hands by the apostles Peter and John. The center lancet summarizes the thematic hope of the iconography by suggesting a final reuniting of the divided body of Christ, through recalling of the first Pentecost when the apostles gathered in the upper room and received the Holy Spirit.

In the center quatrefoil at the top of the tracery is the Jerusalem cross. Depicted in two lower quatrefoils are Orthodox and Celtic crosses, symbolic of ancient streams of Christendom.

War Memorial Chapel

42 FREEDOM (1952)
In honor of all the armed forces who died for freedom 1917-1918
Artists: Reynolds, Francis, Rohnstock and Setti

In the east wall of the chapel the window at the left was given "to honor all the armed forces who died for freedom 1917-1918." The two large figures are St. Michael and George Washington. The smaller panels portray Moses leading the children of Israel across the Red Sea; Martin Luther nailing his historic protests to the door of Wittenberg Cathedral; the United States Marines raising the American flag at Iwo Jima; the Emancipation Proclamation featuring Abraham Lincoln surrounded by slaves with broken chains; and Paul Revere giving his alarm. In the multifoil at the top of the window is the Liberty Bell.

43 FREEDOM (1952)
Memorial: John Upshur Morehead
Artists: Reynolds, Francis, Rohnstock and Setti

The large figures are David as king and Richard the Lion-Hearted. The top medallions show Nehemiah and the rebuilding of the walls of Jericho to make possible again the Jews' freedom of worship, and Elijah barring the way at the entrance of Naboth's vineyard to Ahab and Jezebel. Also shown are the landing of the Pilgrims at Plymouth; a peace council of William Penn and the Indians; an amphibious landing of World War II with a tank emerging from a landing craft; and liberation forces marching through a French city. At the heads of the lancets are the Statue of Liberty and the figure of Freedom from the dome of the Capitol.

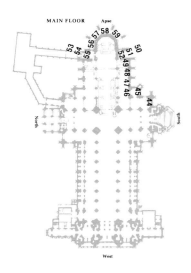

44 SACRIFICE (1952)

Artists: Reynolds, Francis, Rohnstock and Setti

In the center of the large window the supreme sacrifice of all time is represented by the figure of Christ on the cross. Flanking this central figure in the places traditionally occupied by St. Mary and St. John are a modern mother and a young soldier. In the smaller medallions are such figures as St. Ignatius and St. Alban, both martyred; Nathan Hale, who laid down his life for his country; Dr. Jesse Lazear, who sought the cure for yellow fever; four chaplains of World War II fame and the Battle of Midway.

Children's Chapel

45 SAMUEL AND DAVID (1936)

Memorial: Roland Leslie Taylor Jr.
Artist: Henry Lee Willet

David in the right panel represents physical courage. He is shown as he boldly starts out to take food to his older brothers camped against the Philistines. Samuel looks heavenward, David looks forward. In the canopy above, young David conquers the giant Philistine. Directly above his head is an angel with a harp. In the little scene in the bottom background, young David embraces Jonathan while the jealous Saul looks on.

St. John's Chapel

46 MIRACLES OF CHRIST (1931)

Memorial: Marvin Jones
Artist: Lawrence B. Saint
For details, see diagram.

47 MIRACLES OF CHRIST

Memorial: Lucien Jones
Artist: Lawrence B. Saint

48 MIRACLES OF CHRIST

Memorial: Norman Prince
Artist: Lawrence B. Saint

49 MIRACLES OF CHRIST

Memorial: Norman Prince
Artist: Lawrence B. Saint

The Apse Windows

50, 51, 52 THE "TE DEUM" (1932)

Memorial: Mrs Percy R. Pyne
Artist: Earl Edward Sanborn

Two of the largest windows in the cathedral, 65 feet high, carry out the theme of the entire east end of the cathedral interpreting the Te Deum Laudamus from the service of Morning Prayer. The windows are each made up of six lancets rising in three tiers of two. These on the south wall of the sanctuary, to the right of the altar, illustrate "The Holy Church throughout all the world doth acknowledge Thee.."

53, 54, 55 THE "TE DEUM" (1932)

Memorial: Mrs Percy R. Pyne
Artist: Earl Edward Sanborn

The three-tiered "Te Deum" windows on the left of the altar in the north wall of the sanctuary depict apostles, prophets and martyrs.

56 CHILDHOOD OF JESUS (1971)

Artist: Rowan LeCompte

In three lancets the child Jesus is seen at play, throwing a ball to his Mother Mary, studying as he reads the Torah, and at work as he sweeps his father's carpenter shop.
  The window was fabricated by Dieter Goldkuhle.

57 THE CRUCIFIXION (1943)

Memorial: Josephine Wheelwright Rust
Artists: Wilbur H. Burnham and Joseph G. Reynolds

The figure of Christ is suspended on the cross with arms extending across the mullions into the two side openings. In the left lancet is Mary, mother of Christ, and in the right is the figure of St. John the Beloved Disciple. The head of Christ is erect. Above, two diminutive angels hold a crown.

THE MIRACLE WINDOWS IN ST. JOHN'S CHAPEL

46 Window Farthest West

Rosace (red and blue)	
The Syro-Phoenician Woman St. Matthew 15:25	*The Marriage in Cana* St. John 2:1
The Centurion's Servant St. Matthew 8:13	*Healing of the Demoniac in the Synagogue* St. Mark 1:25
Simon's Wife's Mother Healed St. Mark 1:30-31	*The Healing of the Ten Lepers* St. Luke 17:19
Feeding of the Five Thousand (St. Luke 9:10-17) Christ	*Feeding of the Five Thousand* (St. Luke 9:10-17) St. Peter

47 Window Second From West

Rosace (red)	
Christ with Two Fishermen St. Luke 5:4-12	*Christ and St. Peter on or by the Sea* St. Luke 5:4-12
Jesus Walking on the Sea St. Matthew 14:24-36	*St. Peter Walking on the Sea* St. Matthew 14:24-36
Christ Asleep in the Boat St. Mark 4:35-41	*Christ in the Boat With the Disciples* St. Mark 4:35-41
Christ the Fig Tree St. Matthew 21:17-23	*Healing of Man with Dropsy* St. Luke 14:2-7

48 Window Third From West

Rosace (blue and green)	
Healing of Blind Bartimaeus St. Mark 10:46-52	*Healing of the Man Deaf and Dumb* St. Mark 7:31-37
The Paralytic St. Luke 5:17-26	*Healing of the Man at the Pool of Bethesda* St. John 5:8
Healing of the Ear of the Servant of the High Priest St. Luke 22:47-53	*Healing of the Woman with the Issue of Blood* St. Mark 5:25-35

49 Window Nearest Altar

Rosace	
Lazarus being Raised from the Dead St. John 11:1-46	*Lazarus being Raised from the Dead* St John 11:1-46
The Healing of the Daughter of Jairus St. Mark 5:21-43	*The Healing of the Young Man of Nain* St. Luke 7:11-17
The Healing of the Man with the Withered Hand St. Luke 6:6-11	*Healing of the Man Born Blind* St. John 9:1-41

58 CHRIST IN MAJESTY (1943)

Memorial: Harry Lee Rust
Artists: Wilbur H. Burnham and Joseph G. Reynolds

Christ in the central lancet, larger than any other figure and more than twice life size, is majestic and commanding in pose. His right hand is raised in benediction, he holds the orb in his left hand, symbol of divine authority and on his head is the crown of the King of Glory. The whole figure, silhouetted against a glowing ruby background, is enclosed by a decorative vesica.

59 THE RESURRECTION (1943)

Memorial: Gwynn Wheelwright Rust
Artists: Wilbur H. Burnham and Joseph G. Reynolds

Christ in the central lancet stands erect and triumphant holding the blood red banner. At his left St. Michael tramples the dragon. St. Gabriel, herald of the last resurrection, holds the trumpet.

Three windows of the apse, each made up of three lancets, show Christ in Majesty (center) flanked by the Crucifixion (left) and the Resurrection (right)

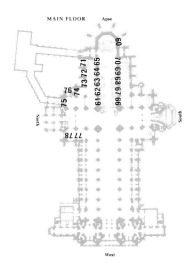

60 THE TRANSFIGURATION (1969)
Memorial: Arthur B. Ambler
Artists: Rowan and Irene LeCompte

At the Transfiguration Peter, John and James saw the inner light of Christ, ordinarily invisible, and this the artists have attempted to suggest through the use of large amounts of transparent glass.

   Christ's feet point to the East and Jerusalem, symbolic of his death. He turns to speak with Moses and Elias, both windblown figures who hover near him. In the opposite lancet Peter represents mankind as he stands astonished, shielding his eyes from the light. James and John are small images in the lower portion of the lancet.

The clerestory windows in the choir depict appearances of angels to men as related in both the Old and New Testaments. All of the choir windows are divided, with the Old Testament references on the north side and New Testament on the south side.

Choir Clerestory (North)

61 ANGEL IN THE GARDEN OF EDEN (1949)
Memorial: Jane James Cook
Artist: Wilbur H. Burnham

The general theme of the window is the dawn of conscience: that moment in history when man acquired free will. The Garden of Eden window (furthest from altar) shows in the central panel the angel standing guard over Eden having banished Adam and Eve, who are seen in the panel just below. The left lancet, reading up, depicts the slow development of life on the planet Earth. The right lancet, also reading up, shows the civilizations created by man with his freedom.

62 ANGEL WRESTLING WITH JACOB (1949)
Memorial: George Hamilton Cook
Artist: Wilbur H. Burnham

The theme is God's search for man and man's for God. In the center lancet, the story of Jacob wrestling with the angel, "until the breaking of the day," is told. Beneath the angel is Jacob's dream of angels at Bethel. The left panel, reading down, shows God speaking to Moses on Sinai; to Saul (St. Paul) on the Damascus road; and to the great scholar and missionary, Schereschewsky, who translated the Bible into Chinese. The right panel, reading up, depicts man seeking God as illustrated by an American Indian, an Old Testament priest of the Temple and a modern celebrant of the Holy Communion.

63 ANGELS OF MINISTRATION—ELIJAH (1981)
Memorial: Katharyn Watson and Ellsworth Chapman Alvord
Artist: Charles Z. Lawrence

The inspiration of the design, found in the first Book of Kings, tells the story of the prophet Elijah who is seen cowering in fear at the voice of God. The left lancet depicts the strong wind and the earthquake; the right lancet with its brilliant reds shows the fire. The window is pivotal in the series of five north choir clerestory windows, harmonizing the blues to the west and the reds to the east.

   The window was fabricated in the Willet Studio, Philadelphia.

64 ANGELS OF DELIVERANCE (OLD TESTAMENT) (1970)
Memorial: Richard Furneaux and Kate Darby Watson
Artists: Rowan and Irene LeCompte

The window is dominated by the central figure, a glorious attenuated angel whose face shows that serene compassion and strength one associates with deliverance. In a bold sweep of line and color the angel's wings dominate the window. One wing is thrust high in the lancet while the other is folded closely about the lower part of the profiled figure.

   In the quatrefoil at the top of the window is the head of a ram with an almost human face. The ram is a symbol of sacrifice and thus relates directly to the right lancet. In the lower portion of the lancet, Abraham kneels facing the angel. At his feet is the knife he dropped when he heard the angel of the Lord tell him he need not sacrifice his son. Above the large bowed figure of Abraham, Isaac stands, surrounded by stars.

   At the top left lancet, Daniel stands with a lion whose jaws have been sealed by the angel. The lion shows quiet strength—a truly peaceful beast. Below Daniel and his lion the flames of Sodom rise above the towers of that doomed city, licking at the heels of Lot as he reaches toward the angel of deliverance.

65 ANGELS OF REVELATION (1979)
Memorial: James S. Hawley
Artist: Rowan LeCompte

The center lancet is dominated by the burning bush in which Moses heard the voice of God. In the upper portion of the right lancet, Moses kneels in awe, staff in hand, before the voice of God. In the left lancet the minor prophet Balaam and his donkey are shown encountering God's messenger. The angelic figure is clad in bright green and carries a large blue sword.

The lower portion of the center lancet depicts Gideon's encounter with an angel.

The figures of this window differ markedly from those in earlier choir windows. God's messengers here do not have wings. In the Old Testament, frequently man did not at first realize he was face to face with a messenger of God. The artist has been faithful to the biblical accounts and has depicted the angels in almost human form.

Choir Clerestory (South)

66 THE ANGEL OF THE ANNUNCIATION (1940)
Memorial: Roland D. and Mary Parsons
Artist: Wilbur H. Burnham

In the window at the south-west end of the choir clerestory Gabriel is seen in the center lancet with the Blessed Mother at the left and her counterpart from the Old Testament, Hannah, at the right.

67 ANGELS OF THE NATIVITY (1962)
Memorial: James Sheldon
Artists: Rowan and Irene LeCompte

The birth of Jesus Christ is symbolized in the center lancet by the great golden angel who raises one hand toward heaven and the other to God. The small tableau above the angel and beneath the tracery depicts Mary holding the child for Joseph to see. Beneath the feet of the golden angel are the shepherds.

A mysterious angel holds and protects the Holy Family during the flight into Egypt in the right lancet. Though the face of Joseph is anxious, Mary is calm and peaceful riding the donkey with the babe in her arms. The incarnation in history is typified by the fact that Christ being truly man had to flee from the wrath of Herod. The lancet tells us that Christ was truly God, and shows John the Baptist baptizing Jesus.

68 ANGELS OF THE RESURRECTION (1934)
Memorial: Leonore Aley Bogy, Ruby Aley Durham and Sarah Aley Hert
Artists: Lawrence B. Saint and Earl Edward Sanborn

Here the angel is seated upon the stone that has been rolled from the entrance to Christ's tomb. Just beneath are the two women with arms uplifted. At the right are two men in shining garments and at the left Mary Magdalene, Mary the mother of James, and Salome, holding in their hands jars of ointment for anointing the body of Jesus.

69 ANGELS OF DELIVERANCE (NEW TESTAMENT) (1934)
Memorial: Mary Lawton
Artists: Lawrence B. Saint and Earl Edward Sanborn

The center lancet shows the angel who delivered St. Paul from the shipwreck, holding a sailboat. At the left is an angel holding broken chains symbolic of St. Peter's deliverance from the prison of Herod. At the right is the deliverance of the apostles from prison when they were jailed by the high priest of the Sadducees.

70 ANGELS FROM THE BOOK OF REVELATION (1934)
Memorial: Annie A. Cole
Artists: Lawrence B. Saint and Earl Edward Sanborn

An angel, beneath whom is the tree of life as described in the Book of Revelation, occupies the center lancet. In the left lancet, around the throne, are the angels whose voices were heard by St. John. The armies of heaven upon their white horses appear in the right lancet.

Detail of Angels of Deliverance window in the north choir clerestory

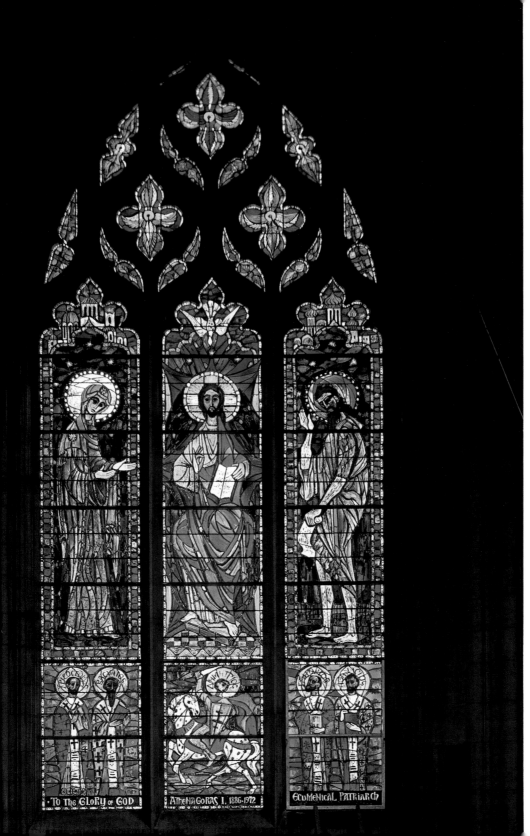

*The Orthodox Stream
of Christianity window in
the east clerestory of the
south transept*

71 Window Farthest East (Red Window)			72 Middle Window			73 Window Farthest West	
The Lost Coin St. Luke 15:3-8			The Rich Fool St. Luke 12:16-22			The Leaven St. Matthew 13:33-34	
The Lost Sheep St. Luke 15:3-8	The Prodigal Son St. Luke 15:11-32		The Pharisee and the Publican St. Luke 18:1-15	The Fig Tree St. Luke 13:6-10		The Sower St. Matthew 13:3-9	The Hidden Treasure St. Matthew 13:14
The Ten Virgins St. Matthew 25:1-13	The Labourers in the Vineyard St. Matthew 20:1-16		The Good Samaritan St. Luke 10:25-38	The Unmerciful Servant St. Matthew 18:21-35		The Tares St. Matthew 13:24-30	The Goodly Pearl St. Matthew 13:45-46
The Marriage of the King's Son St. Matthew 22:1-14	The Great Supper St. Luke 15:16-24		The Rich Man and Lazarus St. Luke 16:19-31	The Unjust Steward St. Luke 16:1-12		The Mustard Seed St. Matthew 13:31-32	The Drag Net St. Matthew 13:47-50

St. Mary's Chapel

71 PARABLES TOLD BY JESUS (1929-30)
Artist: Lawrence B. Saint

72 PARABLES TOLD BY JESUS
Artist: Lawrence B. Saint

73 PARABLES TOLD BY JESUS
Artist: Lawrence B. Saint

Jesus as a teacher is exemplified in these windows. For details, see diagram.

Chapel of the Holy Spirit

74 WOMAN OF SAMARIA AT THE WELL (1935)
Memorial: Henry Yeatman Heyer
Artist: Nicola D'Ascenzo

The only window in the cathedral by the Italian-born artist depicts the woman of Samaria at the well as she offers a ewer of water to Christ.

North Transept
East Aisle

75 STATESMEN (1946)
Memorial: George Shepley Selfridge
Artists: Wilbur H. Burnham and Reynolds, Francis and Rohnstock

The window shows Thomas Jefferson and James Madison as the authors of the Declaration of Independence and the Constitution of the United States.

Medallions included in the design of the window, in addition to those showing the drafting of the Constitution and the Declaration of Independence, portray the laying of the cornerstone of the University of Virginia; a small figure holding the torch of liberty; a President of the United States being sworn into office, his hand on the Bible held by the Chief Justice; the Supreme Court, a group of justices seated around a table and a small figure symbolizing democracy.

76 FLORENCE NIGHTINGALE WINDOW (1938)
Artists: Reynolds, Francis and Rohnstock

In six medallions the window depicts outstanding scenes in the life of Miss Nightingale, including her service in the Crimean War and the founding of St. Thomas Hospital in London.

West Aisle

77 DEBORAH AND BARAK (1933)
Memorial: Amaryllis Gillett
Artist: Lawrence B. Saint

A small window portrays Deborah the prophetess, who judged Israel, and Barak about to sound the horn.

78 MOSES (1933)
Memorial: Sarah Clark Fracker Kauffman
Artist: Lawrence B. Saint

The left lancet portrays the young Moses as he stands in the garb of prince in the court of Pharaoh. At the right he is represented making his appeal to Pharaoh for the release of his people, and in the center he stands on Mount Sinai receiving the Ten Commandments.

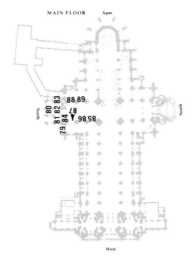

MAIN FLOOR   Apse

North

South

West

79 DANIEL (1937)

Memorial: Harvey Rowland, the Younger
Artists: Reynolds, Francis and Rohnstock

Daniel is shown, at the left, as a young Jewish captive from Jerusalem brought back to Babylon by Nebuchadnezzar. In the center he is represented in the reign of Darius the Persian, and in the smaller panel he stands unafraid and unharmed in the den of lions. In the right lancet that part of Daniel's life in the reign of Belshazzar the Chaldean is represented.

80 THE LAST JUDGMENT (1933)

Memorial: Rose J. Coleman
Artist: Lawrence B. Saint

The north rose window was made by Lawrence Saint in the Washington Cathedral studio. In the center multifoil is the lifesized figure of Christ seated upon the throne of judgment. At the top of the window is the gate of heaven described in the Book of Revelation with the tree of life bearing twelve manner of fruits. Contrasting, at the bottom of the window, is a lake of fire representing hell.

   The petals emanating from the center of the rose portray at the top of the window the parables of the wise virgins as opposed to the parables of the foolish, below. At the upper left, easily recognizable, is a house built upon rock, while at the lower right is a house built upon sand being rent asunder by the storm. In one of the multifoils at the lower right may be seen a man with a millstone about his neck being cast into the sea.

81 FORETELLERS OF JUDGMENT (1935)

Matthew and Joel, Jude and Zechariah
Memorial: Myron T. Herrick
Artist: Lawrence B. Saint

82 FORETELLERS OF JUDGMENT (1935)

Peter and Isaiah, Paul and David
Memorial: James Parmalee
Artist: Lawrence B. Saint

83 FORETELLERS OF JUDGMENT (1935)

John and Jeremiah, Mark and Malachi
Memorial: Matthew Fontaine Maury
Artist: Lawrence B. Saint

84 JACOB'S LADDER (1952)

Memorial: Jessie Woodrow Sayre
Artist: Wilbur H. Burnham

Through the wrought iron gate at the entrance to the north transept balcony passersby can glimpse the small Jacob's Ladder window.

Section of the Florence Nightingale window in the north transept

West Clerestory

85 ENGLAND (1949)
Memorial: Samuel Young and Cora Hull Ramage
Artist: Wilbur H. Burnham

The theme of the English window is the Book of Common Prayer in which Christ is shown as our mediator presenting the prayers of his church before the throne of the almighty. The left lancet symbolizes Morning and Evening Prayer, while in the right lancet the Holy Communion is represented by a kneeling person about to receive the chalice.

86 CANADA (1950)
Memorial: George Carl Fitch Bratenahl
Artists: Reynolds, Francis and Rohnstock

In the central lancet the figure of St. Lawrence holds the gridiron, symbol of his martyrdom. Below him is shown the coat of arms of Canada with the lion and the unicorn. The medallions in the window portray the meeting between the Puritan John Eliot and the Jesuit priest Father Druillets; the Indian girl Sacajawa, who befriended the scouts of the Lewis and Clark expedition; Champlain standing on the deck of his ship; Wolfe, who led the line at the Battle of the Plains in 1759; Sir Frederick Banting, the discoverer of insulin; and William Carpenter Bompas, first Bishop of Mackenzie River, who is shown returning on an improvised raft from a missionary journey.

87 SOUTH AMERICA (1949)
Memorial: James Edward Freeman
Artist: Joseph G. Reynolds

Simon Bolivar, the George Washington of South America, is the central figure. In the left lancet is a figure of San Martin of Argentina, and at the right is Baron do Rio Branco, eminent Brazilian statesman.

East Clerestory

88 PHYSICIANS (1947)
Memorial: Elmer Burkitt Freeman
Artist: Wilbur H. Burnham

Christ, the Healer, is the central figure, flanked on the left by Louis Pasteur and on the right by Sir Wilfred Grenfell of Labrador.

89 LAW (1950)
Memorial: William Edgar Edmonston
Artist: Wilbur H. Burnham

The figures portrayed are Alfred the Great, representing English common law; Moses, the lawgiver from the Old Testament; and Justinian, representing civil law.

Saint Peter and Saint Paul appear in the center window of the three Foretellers of Judgment windows in the north transept

*The north rose in the
north transept above the
three Foretellers of
Judgment windows*

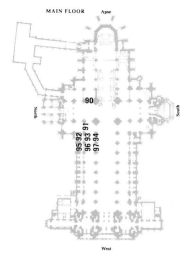

North

South

West

90 EDUCATION (1950)
Memorial: Benjamin DeWitt Riegel
Artist: Wilbur H. Burnham

The principal figure in the central lancet is Jesus as a boy confounding the learned doctors. In the left panel at the top is Plato, and beneath, St. Paul sits at the feet of his teacher Gamaliel. In the right lancet is Horace Mann, chief historical figure in the development of American education, and beneath him the Moravian bishop John Amos Comenius, who introduced new teaching methods in Europe and published the first children's picture book.

91 FISHER OF MEN—ST. PETER (1980)
Memorial: Arthur Kenneth and Esther Louise Jacobs
Artist: Rowan LeCompte

In its depiction of the conversion of St. Peter, the window shows a central figure, Christ, flinging a great golden net over Peter. A corner of the net has been seized by Andrew, one of the first to be drawn to Christ. Andrew in turn indicates Jesus as the Messiah in his gesture to Peter. All three are shown as vigorous, happy people engaged in the hard work that is the lot of fishermen. The strong figure of Peter is seen leaping onto a rock, symbolic of the strong qualities Christ saw in him.

The golden net unifies the window, its filigree-like threads casting a glow of light across the lancets. The artist has used fish as a decoration across the bottom of the window and a fishing boat in the right lancet to help set the scene.

The eastern lancet, which lies in the shadow of the north transept for most of the day, is lightened with the use of gold and silver. LeCompte has attempted to design a window which works harmoniously with the north transept rose window when the two are seen together from the south side of the cathedral.

The window was fabricated in the Greenland Studio, New York.

92 SALVATION FORETOLD—JOHN THE BAPTIST
Memorial: Kathryn Poole Muse Burbank
Artist: Rowan LeCompte (commissioned)

93 JOAN OF ARC (1942)
Memorial: Ethelyn Sarratt Talbot
Artist: Wilbur H. Burnham

The young saint in the center is clad in gleaming armor and a robe of heavenly blue embroidered with gold fleur-de-lis. In the two side lancets, Joan is shown kneeling in her garden listening humbly to the voice promising, "God will help Thee," and again kneeling in Rheims Cathedral at the coronation of King Charles VII. The three panels below symbolize the Battle of Orleans with Joan of Arc mounted upon a white charger.

94 UNIVERSAL PEACE (1940)
Memorial: Frank Billings Kellogg
Artist: Joseph G. Reynolds

One panel of this lovely little window depicts the signing of the Kellogg-Briand peace pact. In the other, soldiers can be seen beating their swords into plowshares.

95 AMOS AND MICAH, THE SECOND COMMANDMENT
Artist: Rowan LeCompte (commissioned)

96 INDUSTRIAL AND SOCIAL REFORM [LABOR] (1959)
Memorial: Philip Murray
Artist: Napoleon A. Setti

The Industrial and Social Reform window depicts the industrial movement and its relationship to working people. Dominating the center lancet is the fearless prophet and builder, Nehemiah. The blueprint in his hand symbolizes man's courage in building. The figure of Moses, in the left lancet, illustrates the progress of people to the Promised Land. In the right lancet the prophet Amos proclaims God's righteousness and judgment—the answer to oppression. Other figures represent those from contemporary life who have proclaimed the need for social reform. The top panel tells the parable of the laborers in the vineyard.

97 HUMANITARIAN (1957)
Memorial: Mabel Thorp Boardman and her family
Artists: Rowan and Irene LeCompte

Represented in the two stained glass windows are six servants of

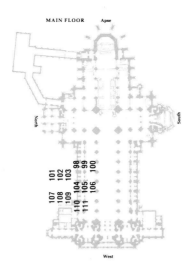

mankind: Elizabeth of Hungary, Father Damien, William Booth, Albert Schweitzer, George Washington Carver and Elizabeth Fry.

98 FAITH OF THE HEBREWS
Artist: Rowan LeCompte (commissioned)

99 AGRICULTURE AND MARITIME (LABOR) (1959)
Memorial: William Green
Artist: Joseph G. Reynolds

The Agriculture and Maritime window depicts the sacramental nature of man's work through the production of food, basic to all life, which leads up to the bread and wine of Holy Communion. Ruth, used as the symbol of agriculture, is shown in the center lancet. In the left lancet are Peter, the fisherman; the fishing boats of New England; gathering grapes in Naboth's vineyard; the making of wine; and the chalice. In the right lancet Joseph is depicted tending his flocks; above is a typical farm scene; and, at the top, an American Indian bakes bread.

100 PRAYER FOR ALL CONDITIONS OF MEN (1957)
Memorial: Henry and Margaret Stuyvesant Rutherford White
Artist: Henry Lee Willet

The windows carry out the theme of peace and universal unity through symbols of the United Nations, the Hague, League of Nations, the peaceful uses of atomic energy, churches of many faiths and peoples of the world at prayer.

101 REFORM AND GROWTH OF ISRAEL
Artist: Rowan LeCompte (commissioned)

102 BROTHER LAWRENCE (1969)
Memorial: Thomas Dresser White
Artist: Patrick Reyntiens

In the right lancet is the centurion who asked Jesus to heal his servant and above is the suggestion of God's mercy. Man's aspiration is depicted in the left lancet as Moses sees the Promised Land and blesses it for God's people. He is supported by Aaron and Joshua. In the cinquefoil at the top is the United States Air Force Academy Chapel. The center lancet tells Brother Lawrence's story of the disillusioned soldier on his way home from battle who sees that the withered trees will bloom again.

103 AMERICA THE BEAUTIFUL (1966)
Memorial: Edwin S. Bettelheim
Artists: Rowan and Irene LeCompte

America the Beautiful is symbolized in color: the four lancets (left to right) represent: the waves of grain and the open skies of the mid-western plains; the autum leaves and wintry forests of the northern states; the fruit trees and blossom of southern orchards; the great red rocks of the south-west and the burning skies of the western desert. The abstract design memorializes the patriotic service of Colonel Bettelheim, especially the "Massing of the Colors" which he instituted at Washington Cathedral.

104 SUFFERING AND REDEMPTION
Artist: Rowan LeCompte (commissioned)

105 SERVANTS OF GOD (1975)
Memorial: William Pratt
Artist: Patrick Reyntiens

The English Quaker William Penn, the central figure in the left lancet, is dressed in traditional Quaker costume. A roundel below shows Penn signing a treaty with an Indian chief. In the center lancet Stephen Langton, Archbishop of Canterbury, is portrayed wearing an Episcopal mitre, green chasuble and Papal pallium. The roundel below shows King John signing the Magna Carta with Langton and several barons standing by. Chief Justice John Marshall of the United States Supreme Court is the major figure in the right lancet. In the roundel are two judicial figures.

106 NATIONAL CATHEDRAL ASSOCIATION (1965)
In honor of: The devoted women of the NCA
Artist: Ervin Bossanyi

From left to right the windows depict the roles of Christian women as: lifegiver, healer, purifier and teacher. Symbolic of the role of woman as purifier is the figure in the lower part of the third lancet as she washes clothes in a stream. Bossanyi's figures

Prayers for All Conditions of Men in the north outer aisle of the nave

of women and children have a Biblical feeling in their simplicity. In the role of teacher, the woman in the center of the right lancet whispers in the child's ear as she points upward to the heavens.

107 TIME AND HISTORY—REBEKAH, JACOB, RACHEL, JOSEPH AND THE TWELVE TRIBES OF ISRAEL
Artist: Rowan LeCompte (commissioned)

108 PHILOSOPHERS (1978)
Memorial: Charles Dyer Norton II
Artist: Rowan LeCompte

The design comes from a concept of Dean Sayre's: Man's search for knowledge moves from the rational (embodied by Socrates in the left lancet) to the discernment of truth through revelation (embodied by Christ on the right). Socrates is presented propounding the nature of truth and right behavior. Four pre-Socratic philosophers hold symbols for air, fire, water and earth.

The window was fabricated in the Greenland Studio, New York.

109 THE TWENTY-THIRD PSALM (1970)
Memorial: Hanson Lee Dulin and Eugenia Bell Dulin
Artist: Albert Birkle

Reading from left to right, the first lancet depicts the second verse of the psalm. The artist shows a shepherd with his crook and several sheep. In the glowing quatrefoil at the top is the Star of David. The second lancet illustrates the fourth verse, with two skulls and a snake as traditional symbols of death and evil. The presence of God in the valley is symbolized by the hand in an aureole at the top of the lancet.

The fifth verse is illustrated to the right of the stone wall that divides the bay. Three persons are seated at the table of God, each with a goblet. The hands of one man are raised in thanksgiving.

In the last lancet two persons are in the temple singing praise to the almighty. The menorah and the harp signify the temple and music. In the quatrefoil above this pair of lancets are the tablets of the Ten Commandments with the symbols Alpha and Omega.

110 THE COVENANT—MOSES, AARON AND JOSEPH
Artist: Rowan LeCompte (commissioned)

111 WOMEN OF THE BIBLE (YOUNG WOMEN'S CHRISTIAN ASSOCIATION) (1977)
Artist: Brenda Belfield

The window depicts the lives of women whose service and work for social change have exemplified the "barrier-breaking love

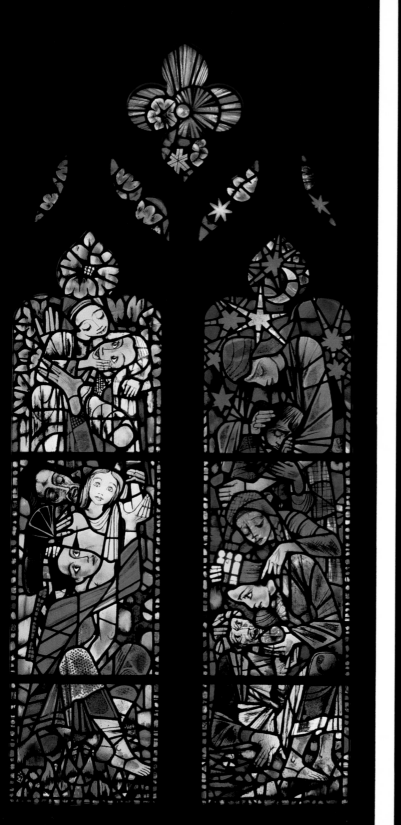

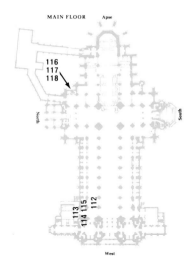

of God." In the window are the New Testament sisters, Martha and Mary of Bethany; Naomi and Ruth; the pharaoh's daughter discovering baby Moses in his basket along the Nile; and symbols of human traits represented by the YWCA motto: "Body, Mind and Spirit."

The window was fabricated by Dieter Goldkuhle.

112 FROHMAN BAY (1982)

Memorial: Roger Stanley and Mary Davis Firestone
Artist: Hans Kaiser

The three-lancet window was the last work of German stained glass artist Hans Kaiser who died in 1982. The most dramatic impression, in addition to the use of color, is made by the heavy, imaginative use of leadwork. The lancets contain smaller pieces of glass than any other window in the cathedral. The window should also be viewed from the exterior to receive the full impact of the workmanship.

113 NOAH (1983)

Memorial: Roger Stanley Firestone, Mary Davis and Peter Stanley Firestone
Artist: Rowan LeCompte

In the sixth chapter of Genesis the earth is described as "corrupt and full of violence," and that is how it is depicted in the left lancet. The center lancet shows a huge wave rolling over the glass, symbol of the flood with which God washed the world clean. God asked Noah, "a righteous man," to build an ark to ride out the flood. The animals can be seen peering out of the ark, the rainbow glowing overhead. The right lancet shows Noah's son, Shem, beginning to till the soil. In the multifoil at the top, a dove carries a sprig of green.

The glass was painted by Richard Avidon and the window was fabricated in the Greenland Studio, New York.

114 THE AGONY OF CIVIL WAR (1979)

Memorial: Robert Todd Lincoln, Mary Lincoln Isham, Lincoln Isham
Artist: Robert Pinart

The abstract window suggests the conflict between the states of the union, the dark reds standing for the battles of the Civil War and the assassination of President Lincoln. Above the reds are the blues and greys of the combatants' uniforms. The yellows and golds at the top of the window suggest fields of wheat and corn and the return of peace. The window was fabricated by Dieter Goldkuhle.

115 LINCOLN'S MOTHER AND STEPMOTHER (1976)

Gift of: Dr. Lent Johnson in thanksgiving for adopted children
Artist: Brenda Belfield

The single lancet window, high on the east wall of the Lincoln Bay, is devoted to the women who brought Abraham Lincoln into life and up to manhood—his mother Nancy Hanks Lincoln and his stepmother Sarah Bush Lincoln. Nancy Hanks wears a pioneer bonnet. The Bible in her hands symbolizes her intellectual nature. Below is the flower of the deadly snakeroot plant responsible for her death, the death of her parents and of many early settlers.

The log cabin, Conestaga wagon and various aspects of pioneer life symbolize the family's part in great westward movement. Young Abe chops wood and his stepmother Sarah Bush Lincoln rests her hand on his shoulder suggesting her gentle, affectionate nature.

Parclose Stairway

116 and 117 TRUTH AND FALSEHOOD (1936)

Memorial: William Thomas Hildrup Jr.
Artist: Lawrence B. Saint

In the parclose stairway leading from the arcade level to the crypts below, these two windows can be seen at close range. They are considered to be Lawrence Saint's masterpieces. As in the north rose window, Saint worked from life to assure the greatest realism possible for his figures.

118 THE GOOD SHEPHERD (1948)

Memorial: Thomas Oliver and Fanny Randle Stokes
Artist: Henry Lee Willett

This is the third window on the parclose stairwell on the way to the north crypt. David is seen at the base of the window, below the Good Shepherd. The notes of the Twenty-Third Psalm, as sung by the Choir of Boys and Men, can also be seen.

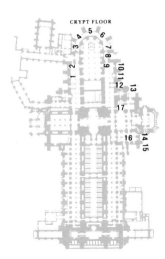

CRYPT FLOOR

Windows of the Crypt
North Crypt Aisle

C1-2 SAMUEL and DAVID; DANIEL and MALACHI (1912)
Artist: John Lisle

Two small windows representing messianic prophets are among the earliest in the cathedral. They were fabricated by Thomas Kempe and Company, London.

Bethlehem Chapel

C3-4-5-6-7 GENEALOGY, GLORIA IN EXCELSIS, ANNUNCIATION, EPIPHANY, NUNC DIMITTIS (1912)
Artist: John Lisle

The five apsidal windows of the chapel were designed to represent the principal scenes attendant to the Incarnation of the Son of God to which the chapel is dedicated. From left to right they depict the genealogy of Christ, the Gloria in Excelsis proclamation to the shepherds, the Annunciation, the Epiphany and the Nunc Dimittis (Simeon's acknowledgement of the Holy Child). All five windows were the work of John Lisle of Thomas Kempe and Company, London.

South Crypt Aisle (Vestibule)

C8 RESURRECTION (1950)
Memorial: Richard and Jean W. Thickens
Artist: Joseph G. Reynolds

This glowing window is set in the wall of the south vestibule, just inside the Way of Peace doorway which is the main entrance to the Bethlehem Chapel from the south roadway.

C9-10-11 JOHN THE EVANGELIST, ABRAHAM and ISAAC, MOSES and JOSHUA (1912)
Artist: John Lisle

Three small windows representing messianic prophets, all were fabricated by Thomas Kempe and Company of London.

C12-13 ONE HUNDREDTH PSALM (1950)
Memorial: Margaret Sturgis Suter
Artist: Wilbur H. Burnham

Two small single lancet windows are behind the wrought iron gate which leads from the south crypt aisle to one of the turret staircases. The only one visible to visitors is the south lancet which symbolizes music. It contains a quotation from the One Hundredth Psalm: "Serve the Lord with gladness and come before his presence with a song." The east wall lancet is purely decorative and allows light to fall in a stream of color into the stairway area. Two symbols, the phoenix, representing resurrection, and a flower, the marguerite, are included in the design.

Ante-Chapel of the Resurrection

C14-15-16 EASTER (1954)
Memorials: Maude Beall Ford (south wall, east window); Raymond MacDonald Yarborough (south wall, east window); Edward G. Drake (west wall).
Artists: Reynolds, Francis, Rohnstock and Setti

The underlying theme of all three windows centers around Easter morning.

C17 RESURRECTION CHAPEL ALTAR WALL
Memorial: William Franklin Draper
Artist: Hildreth Meiere

The resurrection is portrayed in a mosaic above the altar. The risen Christ, robed in white, bears in his hand the cross and banner of victory. Golden rays of the rising sun radiate against the brilliant blue sky behind him. At the right are two Roman soldiers, sleeping, while at the left an angel kneels before the open tomb. William Franklin Draper was a general in the Union Army. The mosaic is framed by the chancel arch, composed of a series of half-circles, each one different from the others.

RESURRECTION CHAPEL MOSAICS (1971)
In the arches on the walls of the chapel nave are a series of modern mosaics portraying the appearances of Christ after his resurrection.

*The Young Women's
Christian Association
window*

C18 RESURRECTION CHAPEL

Memorial: Pinckney Alston Trapier
Artists: Rowan and Irene LeCompte

The panel closest to the sanctuary depicts the appearance to Mary Magdalene. The bright golds of the mosaic denote early morning. The garden is indicated with flowers in dots of color suggesting the freshness of spring. Behind the figure of Christ is the empty tomb, the red stone moved from its entrance.

C19 RESURRECTION CHAPEL

Memorial: Anastasie Caliounghi Groz
Artists: Rowan and Irene LeCompte

The second mosaic depicts Cleophas and his wife Mary on the road to Emmaus. In the lower area the artists show the stranger as he starts to leave them and Cleophas reaches out to restrain him.

C20 RESURRECTION CHAPEL

Memorial: Clarence Louis Tibbals
Artists: Rowan and Irene LeCompte

Next is the appearance in the upper room. At the center of the design, Christ is depicted in dramatic and vibrant color. His dark cloak, symbol of the grave, is pierced by the radiance of his tunic beneath. The action of the composition is supplied by Cleophas and his wife, who have just come from the road to Emmaus. They are describing their own encounter with Christ on the road. While they are speaking, the risen Christ suddenly stands in their midst. At his request for food, one of the disciples offers him a plate with a piece of fish and some honeycomb.

C21 RESURRECTION CHAPEL

Memorial: Peter Anson Ridings
Artists: Rowan and Irene LeCompte

The fourth panel depicts Christ's appearance to Thomas in the upper room. In this panel the artists have caught the moment of confrontation between Thomas and Christ. The focal point is Thomas kneeling before his risen Lord. At the top of the panel are found tables and some of the women bringing food to them. One of the disciples brings lilies, symbolic of eternal life, to decorate the tables.

C22 RESURRECTION CHAPEL

Artists: Rowan and Irene LeCompte

The fifth panel shows Christ's appearance to the disciples as they fished in the Sea of Tiberias. He is seen standing on the shore looking out over the water as he tells the disciples to cast their nets on the other side of the boat. The mosaic is enriched with an interesting and decorative border design, as are all of the panels.

C23 RESURRECTION CHAPEL

Memorial: Irene Matz LeCompte
Artist: Rowan LeCompte

The sixth panel completes the accounts of post-resurrection appearances, portraying Christ on the mountaintop. He is no longer in the midst of his disciples but is withdrawn a little. In the last chapter of St. Matthew's Gospel, the disciples went to a mountain in Galilee where Jesus appeared to them for the last time. There he charged them to go into all nations preaching and baptizing.

LeCompte has placed the figure of Christ at the top left of the panel. Beneath him are representative apostles with their individual symbols: James, the scallop shell; Bartholomew, the knife; Simon, the saw; Peter, the inverted cross; Philip, the Tau cross; Thomas, the builder's T-square; Paul, with the epistles he wrote to the early churches.

The mosaic is literally crowded with other figures, symbolizing the races of the world and Christians throughout the centuries. No one figure portrays a specific culture or race, but together they represent all mankind.

This final panel, completed by LeCompte after his wife's death, is dedicated to the memory of Veronica Irene Matz LeCompte. Venetian Art Mosaics, Inc., performed the fabrication and installation of all six panels, under the supervision of the artist.

Detail of abstract Firestone memorial window in Frohman bay

BIOGRAPHIES OF ARTISTS AND CRAFTSPEOPLE

BRENDA W. BELFIELD was born in Rhode Island, graduated from Holton-Arms School and earned her B.A. in Art Education in 1960 from George Washington University, Washington, DC. She did graduate work at the Corcoran Art School and in 1970 studied glass design and painting with Rowan LeCompte. She lives in Reston, Virginia, and works in her studio in Alexandria. Dieter Goldkuhle is responsible for the selection and fabrication of glass for all her windows. She designed twenty two windows for the towers of St. Peter and St. Paul and has completed many turret windows in both west towers.

ALBERT BIRKLE lives and works in Salzburg, Austria. His windows are fabricated by Derix Studios, Rottweil, West Germany, and by Franz Mayer and Co. of Munich, West Germany. Birkle came to stained glass after he had already established a reputation as a portrait painter. Many of his frescoes and murals are in Salzburg and the surrounding district.

ERVIN BOSSANYI was born in Hungary in 1891 and died in England in 1975. During World War I he was interned in France for five years. Later he settled in Germany where he entered a period of intense, versatile creativity in glass, painting, ceramics, frescoes and sculpture. In 1934 he fled from Leipzig to England where he established his reputation as a master of stained glass. Glass for the Wilson Bay in Washington Cathedral was eight years in preparation in England where Bossanyi made all his windows single-handedly by the traditional medieval process, firing the glass in a small kiln he had built in his garden. His greatest work grew out of personal suffering and tragedy and he poured his life and soul into a plea to mankind to turn the world into a community of love and mutual understanding. His windows are to be found in the sanctuary of Michaelhouse Chapel, Natal, South Africa; St. Gregory's Chapel, Canterbury Cathedral; in London, at the Tate Gallery, the West End Synagogue, the University of London Senate House and Uxbridge Underground Station; at York Minster and at the Ohlsdorf Crematorium, Hamburg, Germany.

WILBUR H. BURNHAM was born in Boston in 1887 and died in 1974. He studied at the Massachusetts School of Art and worked in the Cambridge studio of Harry Goodhue from 1904 to 1908. In 1922 Burnham formed his own company in Boston and continued as an individual designer and craftsman until his retirement in 1968. In 1947 he received the Craftsmanship Medal of the American Institute of Architects for his distinguished work in stained glass.

Burnham's windows are in St. John the Divine and Riverside Church, New York City; he designed the great west window of St. Mary's Redford Church, Detroit, the nave aisle windows of Princeton University Chapel, the windows of the Church of St. Vincent de Paul in Los Angeles and the windows and murals in St. Mary's Cathedral, Peoria, Illinois. He collaborated with his contemporary, Joseph Reynolds, on the south rose window in Washington Cathedral. In their youth the two men had been considered the outstanding exponents of traditional stained glass design and they were among the early artists whose work was commissioned by the cathedral.

NICOLA D'ASCENZO was born in Terricella, Italy, in 1868, and came to the United States at the age of eleven. He studied at the Pennsylvania Academy of Fine Arts and the Philadelphia Museum School of Industrial Arts and operated his stained glass studios in Philadelphia from 1896 until his retirement in 1930. He died in 1954. Descended from a long line of Italian armor makers, D'Ascenzo was the first stained glass artist in America to get the deep, rich effect of the blues and rubies of early medieval windows. The best known of his works are the windows in the Memorial Chapel at Valley Forge, Pennsylvania, begun in 1914.

DIETER GOLDKUHLE was born in 1938 in Widenbrueck, West Germany. He came to the United States in 1962. Goldkuhle holds a "Diploma of Stained Glass Artisan" from the State Glassmaking School of Rheinbach. From 1958 to 1966 he was a journeyman in stained glass studios in Germany, Austria, Switzerland,

53

London and New York. Since 1966 Goldkuhle has worked as a free-lance maker and restorer of stained glass windows at his studio in Reston, Virginia. In Washington Cathedral he has made or installed approximately sixty-five windows in collaboration with artists Brenda Belfield, Albert Birkle, Ervin Bossanyi, Hans Kaiser, Irene and Rowan LeCompte, Rowan LeCompte, Robert Lewis, Robert Pinart, Eduard Renggli, Patrick Reyntiens and Rodney Winfield. He has restored medieval glass in The Cloisters, New York; the Walters Art Gallery, Baltimore and the National Collection of Fine Arts, Smithsonian Institution, Washington, D.C.

MELVILLE GREENLAND, president of the Greenland Studio in New York City, was born in Schenectady, N.Y., in 1925 and studied the art of stained glass with Professor Augustus Annus at the City College of New York. He served his apprenticeship at the Anton Jacobsen Studio, Brooklyn, and the Payne-Spiers Studio, Paterson, N.J. Since 1962 he has been responsible for the fabrication and installation of many windows in the cathedral in collaboration with such artists as Rowan and Irene LeCompte and Benoit Gilsoul. In 1976 he and Dieter Goldkuhle were responsible for the installation of Rowan LeCompte's West Rose window. Since 1976 the Greenland Studio has worked with LeCompte on the nave clerestory windows: Ruth, Abraham, St. Peter, Isaiah, Jeremiah, Noah and St. Paul.

EVIE HONE was born in Ireland in 1894. From the age of twelve years until her death in 1955 she suffered from polio. "The Healing Grace of Christ" window is the only example of Evie Hone's work in the United States. Ten of her windows in England, including those at Eton College Chapel, were designed to replace stained glass damaged in World War II. In Ireland there are forty Hone windows. Her work is known for its rich, deep colors, somewhat reminiscent of the art of the Byzantine period. At the same time, it is quite modern, possibly influenced by Rouault.

HANS KAISER was born in Germany in 1914 and died in 1982. The son of a master silk weaver, he was completely self-taught as a painter and did not see the works of any modern masters until after World War II. He was known as a magnificent colorist before he branched out into stained glass in the late 1950's. Examples of his stained glass can be seen in Soest Cathedral and in St. Boniface Church in Dortmund, West Germany. The Dickinson window was fabricated by Otto Peters, of Paderborn, West Germany, and the Firestone window by Derix Studios, of Rottweil, West Germany.

CHARLES Z. LAWRENCE grew up in Newton, New Jersey, and was apprenticed to the R. H. Buenz Studios of Stained Glass in Newton. He studied for two years at Pratt Institute, New York and

John Wesley, founder of Methodism, appears in a turret window

54

In Memory
Anna Eisenmenger
1874-1955

すずき ひび
1903-1975

Three turret lancets

Industrial and Social Reform (Labor) window

joined the Willet Stained Glass Studios in Philadelphia in 1967. Lawrence is now working as an independent artist in Philadelphia.

IRENE MATZ LECOMPTE was born in 1926. After her marriage to Rowan LeCompte in New York in 1952 she continued her career as an artist in collaboration with her husband, designing and restoring stained glass windows for many churches throughout the United States. Examples of their early work together can be found in St. Matthew's Episcopal Cathedral, Laramie, Wyoming. Irene LeCompte did most of the line painting, if the window was to have figures, and much of the leading; Rowan LeCompte did most of the designing, cartooning and selected and cut most of the glass. They both climbed the scaffolding, one inside and one outside, when installing the finished window.

Their first large combined effort on the close was a window for the refectory of the College of Preachers installed in 1953. One of the most important restorations they undertook was the thirteenth century St. Vincent windows from the Abbey of St. Germain des Près, Paris, now in the Walters Art Gallery, Baltimore. The Angels of Deliverance window (64), installed in 1970, was their last collaboration before her death. She had worked with her husband on the first five of a series of six mosaics in the Resurrection Chapel. The sixth was completed by Rowan LeCompte in her memory.

ROWAN LECOMPTE was born in Baltimore, Maryland, in 1925. He has known Washington Cathedral since 1939 when as a youth of fourteen he fell in love with it. He is primarily self-taught, having read, observed and studied from an early age everything available on the subject of stained glass. In 1941 the cathedral architect, Philip Hubert Frohman, gave LeCompte his first commission: two small windows which are in St. Dunstan's Chapel beneath the south transept steps, an area not open to visitors. In the following two years, still very young, LeCompte designed and made a small window for Trinity College Chapel, Hartford, Connecticut, and five windows for the Episcopal Church of the Incarnation in Baltimore.

In 1945, on his return from service in Europe with the United States Army, LeCompte studied painting with Ben Benn in New York and attended the New School; later he studied at the American University and the Institute of Contemporary Arts in Washington, DC. He married Irene Matz in 1952 and collaborated with her in designing and restoring stained glass windows until her death in 1970. Rowan LeCompte is continuing his work on the clerestory windows of Washington Cathedral, having already completed several. His most famous window is the cathedral's west rose.

ROBERT LEWIS was born in Baltimore in 1925. He studied at the Maryland Institute, the New School (New York), American University and the Institute of Contemporary Arts in Washington, DC. Since 1959 he has been a scientific illustrator at the Natural History Museum of the Smithsonian Institution. A number of Lewis's windows are in St. Albans School and Chapel.

ANTHONY MAKO received his art education at the Industrial Art School of Budapest, Hungary, and stained glass training at Budapest Art Glass Studio. He came to the United States in 1951 and joined the Willet Stained Glass Studios, Philadelphia, in 1958.

ROBERT PINART was born in Paris in 1927, graduated from the École Nationale Supérieure des Arts Décoratifs in 1943 and studied at the École des Beaux-Arts in Paris. He began his training in the French stained glass studios of Max Ingrand, Labouret and Barillet where he worked on the massive restoration of medieval glass damaged or destroyed during the war years.

Pinart came to the United States in 1951 where he continued to use traditional techniques but found a whole new range of expression in the abstract designs of synagogue art. Among the best known examples of his stained glass are four immense windows in dalle-de-verre in Temple Emanuel, Denver, Colorado, completed in 1959. Pinart has also designed tapestries, ritual objects, vestments as well as fountains in metal and panels of enamel on steel. In addition to his Washington and Lincoln windows and his "white windows" in Washington Cathedral, Pinart is known for his windows in the Protestant Chapel at Kennedy Airport, the "World of Darkness" pavilion window at the Bronx Zoo, the mural Flora of Israel for the Fifth Avenue Synagogue at 62nd Street, New York, and his ninety-foot high Burning Bush window in Temple Shaarey-Zedek in Detroit. In 1983 he completed the stained glass for the entire Cathedral of the Immaculate Conception, Atlanta, Georgia, replacing the glass destroyed by fire when the cathedral was totally gutted.

JOHN PIPER was born in England in 1903. He studied at the Royal College of Art. Since 1925 he has exhibited his paintings in London and his work is included in the permanent collections of the Tate Gallery and the Victoria and Albert Museum. Piper has designed stained glass windows for Nuffield College Chapel, Oxford; the Baptistry of Coventry Cathedral; Eton College Chapel and the King George VI Memorial Chapel, Windsor. Though primarily a painter he has also designed for opera and ballet. The tapestries of the high altar at Chichester Cathedral were made from his design.

EDUARD RENGGLI lives and works in Lucerne, Switzerland, carrying on a tradition of family glassmaking in the studio founded by his grandfather. Renggli's work is in many churches in and around Lucerne. In Switzerland he is known for the design and fabrication of Swiss canton arms and other coats of arms in glass.

JOSEPH GARDINER REYNOLDS was born in Wickford, Rhode Island, in 1886 and graduated from the Rhode Island School of Design in 1907. With Wilbur H. Burnham, Reynolds was an outstanding exponent of the traditional school of stained glass design. He worked as a young man as an apprentice for four dollars a week in the Cambridge, Massachusetts, shop of Harry Goodhue, brother of famed church architect, Bertram Goodhue. He founded and directed the studio of Reynolds, Francis, and Rohnstock in Boston and continued to be active until shortly before his death in 1972.

In 1950 Joseph Reynolds was awarded the Craftsmanship Gold Medal by the American Institute of Architects. He created twenty-four windows for Washington Cathedral including half the glass for the south transept rose window and the lancets beneath. His collaborator on a number of windows, including the south rose, was Wilbur Burnham.

The stained glass art of Joseph Reynolds is represented by important windows in the Cathedral of St. John the Divine, Riverside Church and St. Bartholomew's Church in New York City; Princeton University Chapel, Wellesley College Chapel; the American Memorial Cemetery Chapel, Belleau Wood, France, and the American Church in Paris.

PATRICK REYNTIENS was born in London in 1925. He served in the British Army from 1943 to 1947 and studied at the Edinburgh College of Art from 1947 to 1952.

In his first collaboration with artist John Piper, Reyntiens fabricated three memorial windows for Oundle School in 1954-1956. With John Piper he was responsible for the baptistry window of the new Coventry Cathedral, eight windows in Eton College Chapel and eighteen thousand square feet of glass for the Roman Catholic Cathedral in Liverpool.

Reyntiens is a lecturer and contributor to art and architecture magazines. His book, "The Technique of Stained Glass," is a comprehensive technical summary of the field.

LAWRENCE BRADFORD SAINT was born near Pittsburgh, Pennsylvania, in 1885, the son of J. A. Saint, a landscape painter and silhouette cutter. Lawrence Saint left school at an early age, sold newspapers, and was eventually apprenticed to the J. Horace Rudy studio and the Pittsburgh Stained Glass Company.

He went to Philadelphia in 1905 to study at the Academy of Fine Arts and at the end of two years won the Cresson traveling scholarship which took him to Europe. In 1910-11 a second trip to Europe resulted in a series of watercolor studies which were used to illustrate Hugh Arnold's book, "Stained Glass of the Middle Ages in England and France." Saint worked for eleven years on the glazing of the Bryn Athyn Swedenborgian cathedral and in 1928 was selected to direct Washington Cathedral's stained glass studio at Huntington Valley, near Philadelphia.

Saint set up a glass furnace in his own barn where he eventually worked out thirteen hundred different fomulae — three hundred shades of blue alone. His experiments in recapturing the ruby reds, celestial blues and other vibrant colors of medieval glass makers were successful. His formulae, based on spectroscopic analysis of scraps of 13th century glass, are preserved in the Smithsonian Institution. Saint headed the cathedral's glass studio until it was discontinued in 1933. He died at Huntington Valley in 1956.

EARL EDWARD SANBORN was born at Lyme, New Hampshire, in 1890. He studied painting at the School of the Museum of Fine Arts in Boston and was awarded the Paige European Traveling scholarship for two years' study abroad. He served in France with the army during World War I. On his return he began working with Charles J. Connick in Boston and opened his own stained glass studio there. Sanborn eventually moved his studio to Annisquam on Cape Anne and worked there until his death in 1937. He collaborated with Lawrence Saint on the design, execution and installation of a number of windows in Washington Cathedral.

NAPOLEON A. SETTI studied at Boston Normal Art School and at the Fogg Museum Art School at Harvard. He first designed windows for Washington Cathedral when he was associated with the studio of Reynolds, Francis, Rohnstock and Setti. After 1954 Setti began designing independently as owner of the Setti studio. He strove to transform literal topical data into symbols that absorbed the viewer's attention and used glass as expression rather than decoration.

HENRY LEE WILLET was born in Pittsburgh in 1899, the son of stained glass artists, William and Anne Lee Willet, and died in 1983. He was educated at Chestnut Hill Academy, Princeton University and the Wharton School of the University of Pennsylvania.

In 1930 he became president of the Willet Stained Glass Studios of Philadelphia. In addition to the windows installed by his studio in Washington Cathedral, Willet windows are in the Cathedral of St. John the Divine; the Cadet Chapel, West Point; the Chapel Center of the United Nations; the American Research Hospital in Poznan, Poland; and the Cathedral of Mary Our Queen, Baltimore, Maryland.

RODNEY M. WINFIELD was born in Manhattan in 1925 and attended the University of Miami, Florida, and Cooper Union, New York City. He is a member of Emil Frei Associates of St. Louis, Missouri, and associate Professor of Art at Maryville College of the Sacred Heart, St. Louis. He is best known for his sculpture, paintings, tapestries, mosaics, enamels and silver work.

The Annunciation window in the south choir clerestory

GLOSSARY

AISLE Side of a church nave separated by piers from the nave proper.

APSE The round, or polygonal, termination of the sanctuary of a church.

BAPTISTRY Part of a church containing a font and used for baptismal services.

BAY A division or compartment in the arrangement of the building. Marked by space between pillars.

CAME Slender, grooved rod of cast lead used to hold together panes of glass in a window, especially stained glass.

CINQUEFOIL A figure of five equal segments.

CLERESTORY That portion of the wall rising above the triforium level or roofs of the aisles. It is pierced by windows usually of large size.

CHOIR Part of a church appropriated to the singers; such a part separated from the nave on the one hand and the sanctuary on the other.

CRYPT A vaulted space or passageway beneath a church.

ICONOGRAPHY Illustration by pictures or other visual representations; art representing religious or legendary subjects by conventional images and symbols.

LANCET A pointed arched window of one opening frequently arranged in groups of two to five.

MEDALLION Tablet or panel in a wall or window bearing a figure shown in relief, a portrait or an ornament.

MOSAIC A surface decoration of colored marble or glass chips set in cement to form pictures or patterns.

MULLION A slender, vertical, usually nonstructural bar or pier forming a division between lights of windows, doors or screens.

MULTIFOIL A foil of more than five divisions.

NARTHEX A western porch not entering the church itself; a vestibule leading to the nave of the church.

59

NAVE	The body of the church building in which the congregation sits; derived from the Latin word "navis" meaning a ship because of the resemblance between the roof inside and an inverted hull.
PREDELLA	The step or platform on which an altar is placed; the lowest part of a reredos, immediately above the altar; the lowest part of a stained glass window.
QUATREFOIL	A figure in the form of a cross, or four equal segments of a circle, used in window tracery.
ROSE WINDOW	A round window, with tracery dividing it into sections often called petals. The Gothic rose is a development of the Romanesque wheel window which symbolized Christ as the sun.
ROUNDEL	A circular panel, window or niche; a plain or colored glass disk.
SANCTUARY	The eastern part of a church immediately surrounding the altar.
TESSERA	A small piece of marble, glass or tile cut with a square or rectangular face, used in mosaic work.
TRACERY	A term for the variations of mullions in Gothic windows. Applies also to the geometric systems on wall panels and doors.
TRANSEPT	When churches are built in the form of a cross they have two arms, one on each side of the nave; these are called transepts, north and south.
VESICA	A pointed oval figure typically composed of two intersecting arcs; an aureole of this shape surrounds a representation of a sacred personage.

INDEX OF ARTISTS AND CRAFTSPEOPLE

Numbers refer to windows not pages

TOPICAL INDEX

Numbers refer to windows not pages

The Good Shepherd window in the parclose stairwell leading from the north transept to the crypt

The Canada window in the north transept

NUMERICAL LIST OF WINDOWS

The Creation Rose (west rose) (1)
Rowan LeCompte
The Creation
William Douglas Sloane and Malcolm Douglas
Sloane memorial

The Land is Bright (2)
John Piper
Churchill Memorial

Dickinson (3)
Hans Kaiser
Healing, herbs, plants in pharmacy

Ruth and Naomi (4)
Rowan LeCompte
Earth as shelter: Ruth, Naomi, Boaz; Obed;
olive tree symbolizes fruitful earth
Olive Warfield King memorial

The Founding of a Nation (5)
Washington Bay
Robert Pinart

Washington Bay (6)
Brenda Belfield
Martha Washington, Mount Vernon theme,
Washington coat of arms, quilts

Abraham (7)
Rowan LeCompte
Two major events in Abraham's life: birth of
Isaac; God's command that Isaac become a
human sacrifice; aged Sarah with infant Isaac;
Hagar and Ishmael
Hugh Leander and Mary Trumbull Adams and
John Hillary and Mary Payne Trumbull
memorial

Healing Arts (8)
Charles Z. Lawrence
Order of Hospitalers of St. John of Jerusalem,

Sir William Harvey, Joseph Lister, Walter Reed,
Dr. Charles F. Menninger, Drs. Karl and Will
Menninger, Elisha, Marie Curie, Wilhelm
Roentgen
Charles Frederic Wilson memorial

Religious Freedom in Maryland (9)
Rowan LeCompte
Religious toleration: Methodist Bishop Francis
Asbury, George Fox, Bishop John Carroll,
Georgetown University, Bishop Thomas John
Claggett, Captain John Smith, Maryland flora and
fauna, Ark and Dove
Anna Campbell Ellicott, Charlotte Campbell
Nelson, Ella Campbell Smythe memorial

Time and History—Lineage of Jesus (10)
Rowan LeCompte—commissioned
Jesse, David, lineage of Jesus

Poets and Writers (11)
Rowan LeCompte
Eastern Orthodoxy, Roman Catholicism and
Protestantism; John Chrysostom; Dante Alighieri;
John Milton; St. Bride's Church; Satan
Grace Barclay Adams Howard and Beale Rich-
ardson Howard memorial

Early Missionaries of the Northwest (12)
Henry Lee Willet
Lewis and Clark; animals and flowers of west;
meeting with Sioux; first sight of Pacific
John Clifford Folger and Katherine Dulin Folger
and children memorial

Suffering and Redemption—Job (13)
Rowan LeCompte (commissioned)
Gift of American Legion Auxiliary
Veterans of all wars memorial

Architects and Sculptors (14)
Albert Birkle
King Solomon; Abbot Suger; Sir Christopher
Wren; classical and contemporary sculpture and
sculptors, St. Paul's cathedral, Notre Dame,
Michelangelo

Founders (15)
Rowan and Irene LeCompte
Man's search for God; founders' meeting, Charles
Carroll Glover house; history of cathedral; Wash-
ington, D.C.; Jerusalem cross; Jeremiah, St. Paul
Charles Carroll and Annie Cunningham Glover
memorial

Jeremiah (16)
Rowan LeCompte
Jeremiah, Baruch, Nahum; the fall of Ninevah

Scientists and Technicians (Space) (17)
Rodney Winfield
Lunar rock presented by Apollo XI astronauts

Spirit of Law (18)
Napoleon Setti
Law in human life; Saint Paul; Jewish symbol-
ism; Moses; Ten Commandments
Charles Warren memorial

Psalms (19)
Rowan LeCompte
Thanksgiving, praise, supplication, lamentation;
musicians

Artisans and Craftsmen (Labor) (20)
Joseph G. Reynolds
Housing of Covenant theme: building of Noah's
Art, construction of cathedral; Solomon's
Temple; Christ the carpenter blesses craftsmen;
seals of AFL-CIO unions; Star of David
Samuel Gompers memorial

War and Peace (21)
Ervin Bossanyi
War and peace and the Christian faith
Woodrow Wilson memorial

The First Commandment — Amos, Hosea, Micah (22)
Rowan LeCompte
General Douglas MacArthur memorial

Musicians and Composers (23)
Napoleon Setti
Virgin Mary; Deborah, Star of David; Kyrie; J. S. Bach, R. Vaughan Williams; Agnus Dei musical notation; John Merbecke; Black Americans' contribution to religious composition; St. Gregory
Henry A. Hurlbut Jr. memorial

Lee — Jackson (24)
Wilbur H. Burnham
Careers of two Generals: Robert E. Lee and Thomas J. (Stonewall) Jackson; whole armor of God
Robert E. Lee and Thomas J. (Stonewall) Jackson memorials

Isaiah (25)
Rowan LeCompte
Isaiah, Micah
Florence Heaton Marshall memorial

Religious Painters (26)
Joseph G. Reynolds
Creation; St. Luke, Giotto, Durer, Fra Angelico, Rembrandt
Francis Eudorah Pope memorial

Presbyterian History (27)
Robert Lewis
Presbyterian Church in America; John Knox before Scottish Parliament; John Calvin
Andrew William Mellon memorial

St. Paul (28)
Rowan LeCompte
Edward Loud memorial

Healing Grace of Christ (29)
Evie Hone
Raising of Jairus' daughter; touching Christ's hem; two blind men healed
Margot Garrett de Zuberbuhler memorial

History of Baptism (30)
Wilbur H. Burnham

Symbols of baptism; symbols of Church of Wales; ancient, medieval and modern baptisms; St. Philip; Constantine; St. Francis Xavier; St. Columba; Bishop Brent; Rev. Thomas Mayhew on Martha's Vineyard baptizes Indian
Edward and Rahel O'Fon Davies memorial

Theology of Baptism (31)
Wilbur H. Burnham
Baptism of Christ; seven principle parts of baptismal service; St. Paul; Nicodemus; St. Stephen; Pentecost; woman taken in adultery; Christ resists temptation; St. Peter

Early Church at Jerusalem (32)
Joseph G. Reynolds and Associates
St. Luke; St. James the Less; St. Philip in Ethiopia; martyrdom of St. Stephen; St. Mark; St. Peter baptizes Cornelius; early Christian motif of fish; Japan's symbolic chrysanthemum and seal of Diocese of Virginia represent Bishop Tucker.
Henry St. George Tucker memorial

Roman Catholic Stream of Christianity (33)
Albert Birkle
St. Thomas Aquinas; St. Boniface; Pope Gregory; St. Peter's Basilica, Rome; St. Augustine Hippo; St. Monica; St. Ignatius Loyola
Mary Virginia Martin memorial

Orthodox Stream of Christianity (34)
Albert Birkle
Virgin Mary, Christ in Majesty, St. John the Baptist; Byzantine heritage; fathers of early church: Chrysostom, Basil the Great, Demetrius, Gregory of Mazianzus, Athanasius
Athenagoras I memorial

The Church Triumphant (35)
Joseph G. Reynolds, Wilbur H. Burnham
The Church Triumphant; imagery from Revelations; St. John's vision of throne of God in heaven; winged heads of four beasts symbolize four evangelists; Prodigal Son; St. Stephen, Gabriel, Archangel Michael
Mary G. Kingsland memorial

The Apostles (Bartholomew and Philip) (36)
Joseph G. Reynolds, Wilbur H. Burnham
Mabel Stenwood Emery memorial

The Apostles (Andrew and James) (37)
Joseph G. Reynolds, Wilbur H. Burnham
Lillian M. Oakley memorial

The Apostles (Luke and Thomas) (38)
Joseph G. Reynolds, Wilbur H. Burnham

Anglican Stream of Christianity (39)
Eduard Renggli
St. Augustine, Columba, Archbishop Cranmer; early American Episcopal churchman Phillips Brooks, Venerable Bede; symbols for Matthew, Mark, Luke, John; Canterbury Pilgrims
G. Lewis Jones memorial

Reformation and Protestant Stream of Christianity (40) (commissioned)

Coming Great Church (Ecumenical) (41)
Albert Birkle
Tower of Babel; unity of Holy Ghost; baptized Christians await Holy Spirit; laying on of hands by apostles Peter and John; first Pentecost; Jerusalem; Orthodox and Celtic crosses
Frances Berg Kemmer memorial

Freedom (42)
Reynolds, Francis, Rohnstock and Setti
War Memorial Chapel, east wall, honoring armed forces who died for freedom World War I, 1917-18; St. Michael; George Washington; Moses crossing Red Sea; Martin Luther protesting at Wittenberg; U.S. Marines landing at Iwo Jima; slaves surrounding Lincoln (Emancipation Proclamation); Paul Revere sounding alarm; Liberty Bell; paratroops

Freedom (43)
Reynolds, Francis Rohnstock and Setti
War Memorial Chapel, east wall: King David; Richard the Lion-Hearted; Nehemiah rebuilds Jericho; Elijah bars Ahab and Jezebel from Naboth's vineyard; Pilgrims land at Plymouth; William Penn's peace council with Indians; amphibious landing, World War II; liberation of French city; Statue of Liberty; Capitol dome Freedom figure

Sacrifice (44)
Reynolds, Francis, Rohnstock and Setti
War Memorial Chapel, south wall: Crucifixion flanked by modern mother, young soldier (replacing traditional St. Mary and St. John); St. Ignatius, St. Alban; Nathan Hale; Dr. Jesse Lazear; World War II chaplains; Battle of Midway

Samuel and David (45)
Henry Lee Willet
Children's Chapel: Events in life of David and Samuel; Christ and disciples; loaves
Roland Leslie Taylor memorial

Miracles of Christ (46)
Lawrence B. Saint
St. John's Chapel, farthest west: Syro-Phoenician woman; centurion's servant; Simon's wife's mother healed; feeding the five thousand; marriage in Cana; healing demoniac in synagogue; healing of ten lepers
Marvin Jones memorial

Miracles of Christ (47)
Lawrence B. Saint
St. John's Chapel, second from west: Christ with two fishermen; Jesus walking on sea; Christ asleep in boat; Christ the fig tree; Christ and St. Peter on or by sea; St. Peter walking on sea; Christ in boat with disciples; healing man with dropsy
Lucien Jones memorial

Miracles of Christ (48)
Lawrence B. Saint
St. John's Chapel, third from west: healing of blind Bartimaeus; the Paralytic; healing of ear of High Priest's servant; healing of man deaf and dumb; healing of man at Pool of Bethesda; healing of woman with issue of blood
Norman Prince memorial

Miracles of Christ (49)
Lawrence B. Saint
St. John's Chapel, nearest altar: Lazarus being raised from dead; healing of daughter of Jairus; healing of man with withered hand; healing of young man of Nain; healing of man born blind
Norman Prince memorial

The "Te Deum" (50, 51, 52)
Earl Edward Sanborn
South, right of altar, interprets Te Deum Laudamus: "Holy Church throughout all the world doth acknowledge Thee"
Mrs Percy R. Pyne memorial

The "Te Deum" (53, 54, 55)
Earl Edward Sanborn
North, left of altar, interprets Te Deum Laudamus: apostles, prophets, martyrs
Mrs Percy R. Pyne memorial

Childhood of Christ (56)
Rowan LeCompte
Jesus and Mary

Physicians window in the north transept

The Crucifixion (57)
Wilbur H. Burnham, Joseph G. Reynolds
Christ on the cross; Mary, mother of Christ; St. John; two angels
Josephine Wheelwright Rust memorial

Christ in Majesty (58)
Wilbur H. Burnham, Joseph G. Reynolds
Harry Lee Rust memorial

The Resurrection (59)
Wilbur H. Burnham, Joseph G. Reynolds
Christ; St. Michael; St. Gabriel with trumpet
Gwynn Wheelwright Rust memorial

The Transfiguration (60)
Rowan and Irene LeCompte
Christ with Moses and Elias; Sts. Peter, James, John
Arthur B. Ambler memorial

Angel in the Garden of Eden (61)
Wilbur H. Burnham
Garden of Eden, Adam, Eve
Jane James Cook memorial

Angel Wrestling with Jacob (62)
Wilbur H. Burnham
Jacob; Moses on Sinai; Saul on road to Damascus; Schereschewsky; American Indian; Old Testament priest, modern celebrant of Holy Communion
George Hamilton Cook memorial

Angels of Ministration (63)
Charles Z. Lawrence
Angelic appearances in Old Testament; Elijah
Katharyn Watson and Ellsworth Chapman Alvord memorial

Angels of Deliverance (64)
Rowan and Irene LeCompte
Ram symbolizing sacrifice; Abraham and Isaac; Daniel and lion; flames of Sodom, Lot
Richard Furneaux and Kate Darby Watson memorial

Angels of Revelation (65)
Rowan LeCompte
Burning bush; Moses kneeling in awe; Balaam and donkey
James S. Hawley memorial

The Angel of the Annunciation (66)
Wilbur H. Burnham
Gabriel; Mary; Hannah
Roland D. and Mary Parsons memorial

Angels of the Nativity (67)
Rowan and Irene LeCompte
Birth of Jesus Christ; Mary holds child for Joseph to see; flight to Egypt; John the Baptist baptizes Jesus
James Sheldon memorial

Angels of Resurrection (68)
Lawrence B. Saint, Earl E. Sanborn
Christ's tomb; Mary Magdalene, Mary the mother of James, Salome
Mrs Alvin T. Hert and sisters memorial

Angels of Deliverance (69)
Lawrence B. Saint, Earl E. Sanborn
St. Paul delivered from shipwreck; St. Peter delivered from Herod's prison; release of apostles
Mary Lawton memorial

Angels from Book of Revelation (70)
Lawrence B. Saint, Earl E. Sanborn
Tree of life, angels around throne heard by St. John; armies of heaven on white horses
Annie A. Cole memorial

Parables Told by Jesus (71)
Lawrence B. Saint
(St. Mary's Chapel, farthest east)
The Lost Coin; The Lost Sheep; The Ten Virgins; The Marriage of the King's Son; The Prodigal Son; The Laborers in the Vineyard; The Great Supper

Parables Told by Jesus (72)
Lawrence B. Saint
(St. Mary's Chapel, middle)
The Rich Fool; The Pharisee and the Publican; The Good Samaritan; The Rich Man and Lazarus; The Fig Tree; The Unmerciful Servant; The Unjust Steward

Parables Told by Jesus (73)
Lawrence B. Saint
(St. Mary's Chapel, farthest west)
The Leaven; The Sower; The Tares; The Mustard Seed; The Hidden Treasure; The Goodly Pearl; The Drag Net

Woman of Samaria at the Well (74)
Nicola D'Ascenzo

Woman of Samaria offers water to Christ
Henry Yeatman Heyer memorial

Statesmen (75)
Wilbur H. Burnham and Reynolds, Francis and Rohnstock
Thomas Jefferson and James Madison
George Shepley Selfridge memorial

Florence Nightingale (76)
Reynolds, Francis and Rohnstock
Life of Florence Nightingale

Deborah and Barak (77)
Lawrence B. Saint
Amaryllis Gillett memorial

Moses (78)
Lawrence B. Saint
Moses at Pharaoh's court; appeal to Pharaoh; receiving Ten Commandments
Sarah Clark Fracker Kauffman memorial

Daniel (79)
Reynolds, Francis and Rohnstock
Life of Daniel
Harvey Rowland, the Younger memorial

The Last Judgment (80)
Lawrence B. Saint
Last Judgment; Christ sits in judgment; gate of heaven, tree of life, hell; parables of wise and foolish virgins; house built on rock, house built on sand; man with millstone about his neck
Rose J. Coleman memorial

Foretellers of Judgment (81)
Lawrence B. Saint
Matthew and Joel, Jude and Zechariah
Myron T. Herrick memorial

Foretellers of Judgment (82)
Lawrence B. Saint
Peter and Isaiah, Paul and David
James Parmalee memorial

Foretellers of Judgment (83)
Lawrence B. Saint
John and Jeremiah, Mark and Malachi
Matthew Fontaine Maury memorial

Jacob's Ladder (84)
Wilbur H. Burnham
Jessie Woodrow Sayre memorial

England (85)
Wilbur H. Burnham
Book of Common Prayer
Samuel Young and Cora Hull Ramage memorial

Canada (86)
Reynolds, Francis and Rohnstock
St. Lawrence; coat of arms of Canada; Puritan
John Eliot meets Jesuit Father Druillet; Indian girl
Sacajawa; Champlain; Wolfe; Sir Frederick
Banting; missionary Bishop Bompas
George Carl Fitch Bratenahl memorial

South America (87)
Joseph G. Reynolds
Simon Bolivar; San Martin of Argentina; Baron
do Rio Branco (Brazil)
James Edward Freeman memorial

Physicians (88)
Wilbur H. Burnham
Christ the Healer; Louis Pasteur; Sir Wilfred
Grenfell; country doctor; Red Cross, TB symbols
Elmer Burkitt Freeman memorial

Law (89)
Wilbur H. Burnham
Alfred the Great; Moses; Justinian; Magna Carta,
trial by jury, Constitutional convention
William Edgar Edmonston memorial

Education (90)
Wilbur H. Burnham
Jesus as boy; Plato; St. Paul at Gamaliel's feet;
Horace Mann; Moravian Bishop John Amos
Comenius; little red schoolhouse
Benjamin DeWitt Riegel memorial

Fisher of Men (91)
(St. Peter)
Rowan LeCompte
Conversion of Peter: Christ flings net over Peter;
Andrew; fish, fishing boat
Arthur Kenneth Jacobs memorial

Salvation Foretold—John the Baptist (92)
Rowan LeCompte
commissioned
Kathryn Poole Muse Burbank memorial

Joan of Arc (93)
Wilbur H. Burnham
Joan of Arc in armor, at Rheims Cathedral at
coronation of Charles VII, Battle of Orleans; St.
Michael
Ethelyn Sarratt Talbot memorial

Universal Peace (94)
Joseph G. Reynolds
Kellogg-Briand peace pact; soldiers beat swords
into plowshares
Frank Billings Kellogg memorial

Amos and Micah (95)
Rowan LeCompte
commissioned

Industrial and Social Reform (Labor) (96)
Napoleon A. Setti
Nehemiah; Moses; Amos; parable of laborers
in vineyard
Philip Murray memorial

Humanitarian (97)
Rowan and Irene LeCompte
Six servants of mankind; Elizabeth of Hungary,
Father Damien, William Booth, Albert
Schweitzer, George Washington Carver, Elizabeth
Fry
Mabel Thorp Boardman and family memorial

Faith of the Hebrews (98)
Rowan LeCompte
commissioned

Agriculture and Maritime (Labor) (99)
Joseph G. Reynolds
Sacramental nature of production of food, com-
munion bread and wine; Ruth, Peter, New En-
gland fishing fleet, Naboth's vineyard, Joseph
tends flocks, typical farm scene, American
Indian bakes bread, 4H symbol
William Green memorial

Prayers for All Conditions of Men (100)
Henry Lee Willet
Peace and universal unity
Henry and Margaret Stuyvesant Rutherford
White memorial

Reform and Growth of Israel (101)
Rowan LeCompte

Brother Lawrence (102)
Patrick Reyntiens
Brother Lawrence; U.S. Air Force Academy
Chapel; centurion; Moses, Aaron, Joshua
Thomas Dresser White memorial

America the Beautiful (103)
Rowan and Irene LeCompte
America's regions symbolized in color
Edwin S. Bettelheim memorial

Suffering and Redemption (104)
Rowan LeCompte

Servants of God (105)
Patrick Reyntiens
Quaker William Penn; Stephen Langton, Arch-
bishop of Canterbury; King John; Chief Jus-
tice John Marshall of U.S. Supreme Court
William Pratt memorial

National Cathedral Association (106)
Ervin Bossanyi
Roles of Christian women: lifegiver, healer, puri-
fier, teacher
Honoring devoted women of the N.C.A.

Time and History (107)
Rowan LeCompte
commissioned
Rebekah, Jacob, Rachel, Joseph and the twelve
tribes of Israel

Philosophers (108)
Rowan LeCompte
Socrates addresses Athenians; Plato holding
stylus; Christ breaks bread with Cleophas
and wife
Charles Dyer Norton II memorial

The Twenty-Third Psalm (109)
Albert Birkle
Symbolic interpretation: shepherd with crook;
star of David; skulls and snake of death and evil;
God's hand; thanksgiving; menorah and harp;
tablets of Ten Commandments; Alpha and Omega
Hanson Lee and Eugenia Bell Dulin memorial

The Covenant (110)
Rowan LeCompte
commissioned
Moses, Aaron and Joseph

Women of the Bible (111)
Brenda Belfield
Martha and Mary of Bethany; Ruth and Naomi;
pharaoh's daughter with infant Moses; motto,
"Body, Mind, Spirit."
Young Women's Christian Association

Frohman Bay (112)
Hans Kaiser
Abstract window
Roger Stanley and Mary Davis Firestone
memorial

Noah (113)
Rowan LeCompte
Corrupt and violent earth; cleansing flood;
Noah and ark; animals and rainbow; Shem tills
soil; dove of peace
Roger Stanley Firestone, Mary Davis and Peter
Stanley Firestone memorial

The Agony of Civil War (114)
Robert Pinart
Abstract window
Robert Todd Lincoln, Mary Lincoln Isham
and Lincoln Isham memorial

Lincoln's Mother and Stepmother (115)
Brenda Belfield
Nancy Hanks and Sarah Bush Lincoln

Truth and Falsehood (116) (Parclose)
Lawrence B. Saint
Truth: Christ according to St. John, Thomas,
Nicodemus
William Thomas Hildrup Jr. memorial

Truth and Falsehood (117) (Parclose)
Lawrence B. Saint
Falsehood: Pilate, Peter, Judas, Caiaphas
William Thomas Hildrup Jr. memorial

Good Shepherd (118) (Parclose stairwell)
Henry Lee Willet
Shepherd, David, notes of 23rd Psalm
Thomas Oliver Stokes and Fanny Randle Stokes
memorial

North Crypt Aisle (C1-2)
John Lisle
Thomas Kempe and Co., London
Messianic prophets: Samuel and David, Daniel
and Malachi

Bethlehem Chapel (C3-4-5-6-7)
John Lisle
Thomas Kempe and Co., London
Genealogy of Christ, Gloria in Excelsis, Annun-
ciation, Epiphany, Nunc Dimittis

Resurrection (C8)
Joseph G. Reynolds
Richard and Jean W. Thickens memorial

South Crypt Aisle (C9-10-11)
John Lisle
Thomas Kempe and Co., London
St. John the Evangelist; Messianic prophets:
Abraham and Isaac; Moses and Joshua

Scientists and Technicians (Space) window in south nave aisle

South Crypt—One Hundredth Psalm (C12-13)
Wilbur H. Burnham
Music, 100th Psalm, resurrection, flower
Margaret Sturgis Suter memorial

Easter
Crypt ante-chapel of Resurrection (C14-15-16)
Reynolds, Francis, Rohnstock and Setti
Maude Beall Ford, Raymond MacDonald
Yarborough, Edward G. Drake memorials

Resurrection Chapel Mosaics (C17-18-19-20-21-22-23)
Appearance of Christ after resurrection

Resurrection Chapel Altar (C17)
Hildreth Meiere
Christ risen; rising sun; Roman soldiers sleep; angel before tomb
William Franklin Draper memorial

Resurrection Chapel (C18)
(Panel closest to sanctuary on left of altar)
Rowan and Irene LeCompte
Mary Magdalene appears; Christ in front of tomb;
early morning sun, spring flowers
Pinckney Alston Trapier memorial

Resurrection Chapel (C19)
(Second panel on left)
Rowan and Irene LeCompte
Cleophas and wife Mary on road to Emmaus with
stranger (Christ)
Anastasie Galiounghi Groz memorial

Resurrection Chapel (C20)
(Third panel on left))
Rowan and Irene LeCompte
Christ appears in upper room; Cleophas and wife;
disciple offers food to Christ
Clarence Louis Tibbals memorial

Resurrection Chapel (C21)
(Fourth panel on left)
Rowan and Irene LeCompte
Christ appears to Thomas in upper room;
Thomas kneels before risen Lord; lilies, symbolic
of eternal life, on tables
Peter Anson Ridings memorial

Resurrection Chapel (C22)
(Fifth panel)
Rowan and Irene LeCompte
Christ appears before disciples as they fish; Sea
of Tiberias

Resurrection Chapel (C23)
Rowan LeCompte
Christ on the mountain top; charges disciples to
go forth; symbols of apostles; mankind
represented
Veronica Irene Matz LeCompte memorial

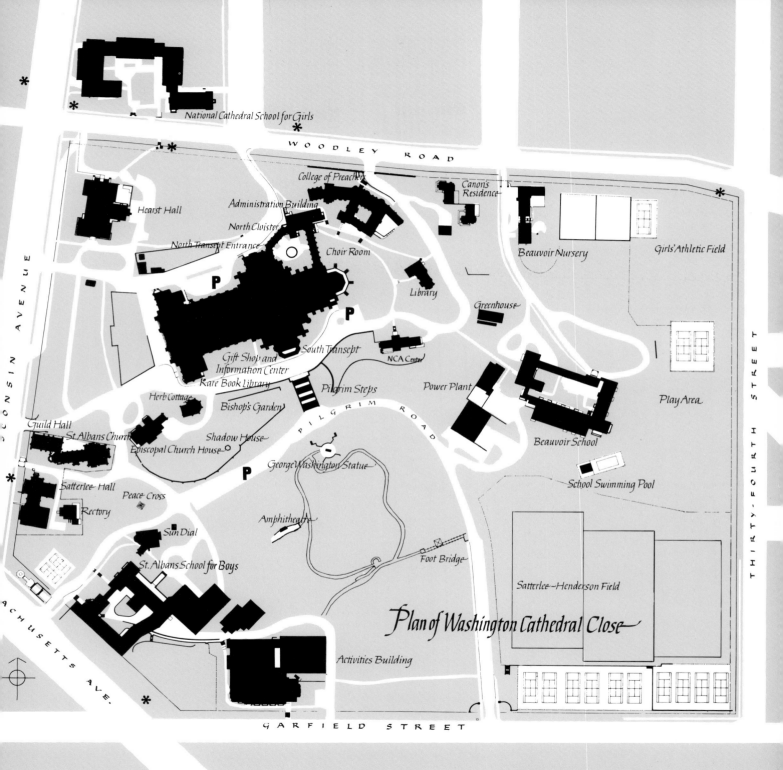

National Cathedral School for Girls

WOODLEY ROAD

College of Preachers

Canon's Residence

Administration Building

Hearst Hall

North Cloister

North Transept Entrance

Choir Room

Beauvoir Nursery

Girls' Athletic Field

Library

P

Greenhouse

P

South Transept

NCA Center

Gift Shop and
Information Center

Rare Book Library

Pilgrim Steps

Power Plant

Play Area

Herb Cottage

Bishop's Garden

Guild Hall

St. Albans Church

Shadow House

Episcopal Church House

Beauvoir School

P

George Washington Statue

School Swimming Pool

Satterlee Hall

Peace Cross

Rectory

Amphitheatre

Sun Dial

St. Albans School for Boys

Foot Bridge

Satterlee–Henderson Field

𝒫lan of Washington Cathedral Close

Activities Building

GARFIELD STREET

WISCONSIN AVENUE

MASSACHUSETTS AVE.

THIRTY-FOURTH STREET

PILGRIM ROAD

* Bus Stop   **P** Parking

THE CATHEDRAL CHURCH OF SAINT PETER AND SAINT PAUL
WASHINGTON CATHEDRAL
MOUNT SAINT ALBAN
WASHINGTON, DISTRICT OF COLUMBIA 20016